District Leader Internship

District Leader Internship challenges school district leader interns to develop a rigorous and broad-based experience to prepare for their first job as a superintendent. This text provides step-by-step guidance for interns, district supervisors, and preparation program faculty to develop, monitor, and evaluate the internship experience. This accessible resource includes activities and assessments, explores how to develop an internship plan, unpacks duties of the intern, supervisor, and advisor, and helps readers prepare a final program report. The content is aligned with the National Education Leadership Preparation (NELP) Standards for district-level administrators and assists in preparation for certification exams and applications for desired superintendency positions.

Gary E. Martin is Professor of Educational Leadership at Lamar University, USA.

Jimmy R. Creel is Assistant Professor of Educational Leadership at Lamar University, USA.

Thomas W. Harvey is Clinical Instructor of Educational Leadership at Lamar University, USA.

Robert E. Nicks is Associate Professor of Educational Leadership at Lamar University, USA.

Michael Schwanenberger is Associate Professor and Department Chair of the Educational Leadership Department at Northern Arizona University, USA.

District Leader Internship

*Developing, Monitoring, and Evaluating
Your Leadership Experience*

Gary E. Martin, Jimmy R. Creel, Thomas W. Harvey,
Robert E. Nicks, and Michael Schwanenberger

NEW YORK AND LONDON

Cover image: © Getty Images

First published 2023
by Routledge
605 Third Avenue, New York, NY 10158

and by Routledge
4 Park Square, Milton Park, Abingdon, Oxon, OX14 4RN

Routledge is an imprint of the Taylor & Francis Group, an informa business

© 2023 Gary E. Martin, Jimmy R. Creel, Thomas W. Harvey, Robert E. Nicks, and Michael Schwanenberger

The right of Gary E. Martin, Jimmy R. Creel, Thomas W. Harvey, Robert E. Nicks, and Michael Schwanenberger to be identified as authors of this work has been asserted in accordance with sections 77 and 78 of the Copyright, Designs and Patents Act 1988.

All rights reserved. The purchase of this copyright material confers the right on the purchasing institution to photocopy or download pages which bear a copyright line at the bottom of the page. No other parts of this book may be reprinted or reproduced or utilised in any form or by any electronic, mechanical, or other means, now known or hereafter invented, including photocopying and recording, or in any information storage or retrieval system, without permission in writing from the publishers.

Trademark notice: Product or corporate names may be trademarks or registered trademarks, and are used only for identification and explanation without intent to infringe.

Library of Congress Cataloging-in-Publication Data
Names: Martin, Gary E., 1949 July 16- author.
Title: District leader internship : developing, monitoring, and evaluating your leadership experience / Gary E. Martin, Jimmy R. Creel, Thomas W. Harvey, Robert E. Nicks, and Michael Schwanenberger.
Description: New York, NY: Routledge, 2022. | Includes bibliographical references and index.
Identifiers: LCCN 2022003898 (print) | LCCN 2022003899 (ebook) | ISBN 9781032283876 (hardback) | ISBN 9781032289861 (paperback) | ISBN 9781003299493 (ebook)
Subjects: LCSH: School administrators—Training of—United States. | School management and organization—Study and teaching (Internship)—United States.
Classification: LCC LB1738.5 .M385 2022 (print) | LCC LB1738.5 (ebook) | DDC 371.2/011—dc23/eng/20220302
LC record available at https://lccn.loc.gov/2022003898
LC ebook record available at https://lccn.loc.gov/2022003899

ISBN: 978-1-032-28387-6 (hbk)
ISBN: 978-1-032-28986-1 (pbk)
ISBN: 978-1-003-29949-3 (ebk)

DOI: 10.4324/9781003299493

Typeset in Palatino
by KnowledgeWorks Global Ltd.

Access the Support Material: www.routledge.com/9781032289861

◼ Contents

Supplemental Downloads

Some of the tools in this book can be downloaded and printed for classroom use. There are also additional resources available that complement the material in the book. You can access these downloads by visiting the book product page on our website, www.routledge.com/9781032289861. Then click on the tab that says Supplemental Downloads and select the files. They will begin downloading to your computer.

◼ Foreword

Standards for school leadership have a history that was based upon the need to better prepare instructionally focused principals, superintendents, and other school administrators. The first coordinated effort to develop standards for educational leadership preparation began with the publication of the Interstate School Leaders Licensure Consortium Standards (ISLLC) authorized by the National Policy Board for Educational Administration (NPBEA) in 1996. This body, for the first time, brought the leading educational leadership professional associations together to compile the academic scholarship and best K-12 practices to establish standards for training school leaders.

In the last 25 years, the National Policy Board for Educational Administration made updates and revisions to the original standards. In 2008 the Educational Leadership Constituent Council (ELCC) and in 2018 the National Educational Leadership Preparation (NELP) standards were published to better reflect and refine educational leadership preparation in key areas of leadership practice within K-12 schools. Each iteration of the standards continued to emphasize current research, scholarship, and best K-12 practice with an emphasis on instructional leadership.

The latest leadership preparation standards for use by university educational leadership preparation programs were published as the National Educational Leadership Preparation (NELP) standards in 2018 (see NELP Standards, 2018). Educational leadership preparation – to match the university focus on degrees (not each state's certification) – designed the NELP standards to reflect general school leadership preparation at the building and central office levels. Thus, there are two sets of NELP standards to guide curriculum development for leadership preparation at the program level. One set of standards – National Educational Leadership Preparation Standards: Building Level were, primarily, designed to reflect pre-service training for building-level leadership at the master's degree level. The National Educational Leadership Preparation Standards: District Level were designed to reflect central office educational Leadership preparation at the Specialist or doctoral degree levels. It is this set of leadership preparation standards – District Level – reflected in *School District Leadership Internship: Developing, Monitoring, and Evaluating Your Leadership Experience.*

The internship is the opportunity to apply the knowledge of the content curriculum. *School District Leadership Internship: Developing, Monitoring, and Evaluating Your Leadership Experience* offers the aspiring school leader insight into the practice of school leadership within a school setting. Standard 8 of the NELP standards describes the intent of the internship of turning applied knowledge as an aspiring leader into informed practice.

Candidates successfully complete an internship under the supervision of knowledgeable, expert practitioners that engages candidates in multiple and diverse district settings and provides candidates with coherent, authentic, and sustained opportunities to synthesize and apply the knowledge and skills identified in NELP Standards 1–7 in ways that approximate the full range of responsibilities required of district-level leaders and enable them to promote the current and future success and well-being of each student and adult in their district. (NELP District Standards 2018, p. 29)

The district-level internship is the culmination of pre-service preparation about leadership at the K-12 school system level. And yet, it is only a window into the applied, practical, political, financial, legal, and relationship-intense world of school leadership at the school district level. One must always recognize the limitations of an internship as a pre-service learning experience to further refine one's own approach to leadership during an era of great change. However, *School District Leadership Internship: Developing, Monitoring, and Evaluating Your Leadership Experience* is the book to help the aspiring K-12 educational leader develop insight into the applied world of schooling. It is, in fact, the reason for this book. The authors have crafted a. book that directly assists the graduate student and aspiring educational leader "to better plan, implement, monitor, and assess their internship experience in preparation for certification, licensure, and advancement into desired district-level leadership positions".

The internship is not only a culminating experience for most educational leadership preparation programs, but a seminal experience. It is an experiential approach to learning that McCarthy (2010) outlined as a "merging of experience, cognition, and behavior" (p. 131). The authors of *School District Leadership Internship: Developing, Monitoring, and Evaluating Your Leadership Experience* present a meaning-making approach to building one's own leadership capacity. It isn't a culminating internship experience as much as it is an experiential approach to a lifetime of learning about educational leadership.

Dr. Jim Berry,
Executive Director of the International Council of Professors
of Educational Leadership (ICPEL)

■ Preface

This text was written to assist the graduate student or educational leadership intern to better plan, implement, monitor, and assess their internship experience in preparation for certification, licensure, and advancement into desired district-level leadership positions. The core of the text focuses on developing a substantial degree of mastery of the national standards for educational leadership which typically are highly correlated with varying state standards. The text serves as a resource for university and non-university preparation programs. Interns must be knowledgeable of and adhere to specific requirements of their university or other preparation program requirements, processes, and expectations, as they may differ from the text.

Outline and Unique Aspects of the Text

The text is organized according to the four stages of an internship – pre-assessment, internship planning, internship implementation, and evaluation of skill development and accomplishments.

Stage 1 covers several necessary personal and school assessments as a starting point for internship readiness. These include:

a. The National Education Leadership Preparation (NELP) Standards Assessment requires the intern to learn and perform initial district leadership skills in a variety of essential contexts. This assessment provides the intern with an understanding of the wide breadth of experience and demonstration of skills to be developed.

b. Self and Superior Dispositions Assessments require the intern to self-assess and plan strategies for improvement according to individual need, experience, goals, and performance expectations. This allows the intern to focus on specific dispositions and areas needing improvement.

c. School District Assessments require the intern to situate internship plans according to district needs, goals, and performance expectations. This allows the intern to serve the district as he/she works on increased learning, overall school improvement, and individual development.

d. Performance assessments. As part of self, school and program assessment of internship performance, the intern will be required to complete one or more performance assessment tasks that demonstrate his or her leadership skills for the preparation program, licensure requirements or district purposes. This will be incorporated into the internship plan and may be presented as work projects, an action research experience or other culminating report or work product.

This background information serves to assist the intern and district supervisor in the following planning stages.

Stage 2 covers the development of the initial internship plan. A variety of examples of intern activities are listed under each of the seven NELP Standards. The intern is NOT required to undertake all the suggested activities listed. The intern, in consultation with the district internship supervisor and program advisor, can choose from these activities or may design other activities related to the standard. In this fashion, the internship plan can be individualized, while ensuring a sufficient broad base of experience and high level of expectation. For each activity, the intern, district internship supervisor, and program advisor will need to determine the intern's responsibilities, degree of independence and supervision, documentation, and leadership skill performance evidence. This stage allows for consensus of the plan by the intern, district internship supervisor, and preparation program advisor.

Stage 3 covers the implementation of the plan and means of documenting and learning through the experience. This section addresses interviewing a variety of school leaders to gain insight into differing organizational departments/areas and acquiring additional relevant intern activities. This stage also requires the intern, while implementing planned activities, to focus on observing theory in practice and reflecting in and on practice. This stage also describes keeping a log and journal and conducting formative evaluation. This stage assists the intern in completing all requirements, work products, and assignments for the final intern evaluation stage.

Stage 4 addresses the final internship professional report or portfolio of work, assessments, and accomplishments. Although preparation programs may require additional or differing final artifacts, the authors suggest completion and presentation of the following:

- Internship Log
- NELP Professional Standards Progress
- Dispositions and Interpersonal Skill Assessment/Progress
- Foundational Leadership Skills Development
- Reflective Practice Outcomes
- Large Feld-based Assignments, Projects, or Action Research
- Impact on Student Learning and/or Learning Environment
- District Improvement Recommendations
- Resume/Vita and Letter of Interest
- Future Professional Development Plan
- Developing a Portfolio

■ Acknowledgments

Special thanks to the co-authors of School Leader Internship for allowing reprints of their research and writing in this book

    Arnie Danzig, Professor Emeritus, Arizona State University
    Margaret Terry Orr, Professor, Fordham University
    Richard Flanary, former Deputy Director, NASSP

Special thanks for writing the Foreword:

    Jim Berry, Executive Director, ICPEL

Special thanks for the guidance and support in publication:

    Heather Jarrow, Education Publisher, Routledge
    Brad Bizzell, ICPEL Publications Director

Introduction

District Leader Internship: Developing, Monitoring, and Evaluating Your Leadership Experience is written to meet the specific National Educational Leadership Preparation (NELP) standards, correlated state standards, and individual school, district, preparation program, and professional goals. The intent is to assist aspiring educational leaders in the assessment, design, implementation, and evaluation of a successful district leadership experience. The term leadership experience is appropriate and signifies a radical departure from the traditional internship and/or district training program, typically based on documenting tasks assigned or hours completed. Instead, the focus here is on the quality of the learning experiences and the nature of leadership skills that the intern develops through them. In using a leadership development approach, the intern assumes the leadership role over their own development. In effect, the leadership experiences become a strategic plan, requiring assessments, timelines, ongoing monitoring and adjusting, evaluation, and reporting.

The internship is both a capstone of an educational endeavor and a beginning experience in meeting the demands of a new position and new role in educational leadership. It is assumed that prerequisite knowledge, skill, and disposition are at an adequate level for entry into a new initial leadership experience. The internship requires a high level of readiness knowledge, skill, appropriate disposition, and effort. Gaining further from the experience of initial leadership and experience is the internship goal. For the internship to be effective, the intern must assume responsibility and take the initiative to create meaningful experiences that build leadership capacity. The intern will develop, refine, improve, and incorporate leadership skills into their repertoire, along with gaining new knowledge and mindsets across a spectrum of school district contexts including various departments, community stakeholders, individual schools, and the larger state and national governing bodies.

School district leaders play a critical role in improving student outcomes, ensuring quality instruction, and the ability to turn around struggling public schools (Scott, 2017). Leaders must first know what they are made of, their strengths, weaknesses, values, and beliefs, and what they wish to become (Bennis, 2003). They must do this, despite other people and events that might be in opposition. The intern becomes accountable for the breadth, depth, and rigor of the experience. True leaders welcome this responsibility and the resulting balance of authority that allows them to accomplish great things. There are virtually no documented instances of troubled school districts being turned around without intervention by an effective leader. Many other factors may contribute to such turnarounds, but leadership is the catalyst (Leithwood et al., 2004).

DOI: 10.4324/9781003299493-1

To Do List

Stage 1: Self and District Assessments

- ◆ Choose the district internship supervisor.
- ◆ Complete the NELP Standards Assessment.
- ◆ Complete the Dispositions Assessment.
- ◆ Obtain and analyze district goals and priorities, recent assessments, and improvement plans.
- ◆ Research the history, traditions, demographics, budget, and current issues and needs of the district.

Stage 2: Developing the Internship Plan

- ◆ Choose activities under each of the seven NELP standards.
- ◆ Choose activities from selected foundational leadership skills.
- ◆ Include any required activities assigned by the university/program advisor.
- ◆ Choose dispositions and interpersonal skills to improve (others added later).
- ◆ Meet with district supervisor and program advisor to reach consensus on the planned activities and discuss potential future leadership activities or project(s) and possible deliverables.
- ◆ Meet with the program advisor for method used to document the internship.
- ◆ Present the plan to the program advisor, if applicable.

Stage 3: Implementing the Internship Plan

- ◆ Implement planned activities and be open to new unplanned opportunities.
- ◆ Decide which individuals to work with and/or observe and/or interview and compile a networking list of these contacts. Add or adapt new activities recommended by interviewees.
- ◆ Keep a log of activities.
- ◆ Reflect on experience during and following intern activities.
- ◆ Monitor and improve dispositions and interpersonal skills.
- ◆ Monitor progress toward skill mastery, particularly as defined by state and national standards.
- ◆ Complete project-related work.
- ◆ Adjust intern activities throughout this stage.

Stage 4: Evaluating the Internship

- ◆ Completed final log and portfolio or report of accomplishments and work completed.
- ◆ Documented progress toward mastery of national and/or state standards.
- ◆ Summarized key learning from experience in reflective practice, and disposition/ interpersonal skill and fundamental skill development.
- ◆ Presented outcomes of independent leadership and the impact on student learning or the learning environment.
- ◆ Compiled a prioritized list of school/district improvements and recommendations.
- ◆ Updated the resume/vita; compose letter of interest; and develop a future professional development plan.
- ◆ Presented the Final Internship Report to the school internship supervisor and/or program advisor.

Assessing the Intern and Field Experiences

Key to learning in the internship is assessment and feedback from self-evaluations, internship supervisors, and preparation program faculty and advisors. It is highly recommended that interns and their programs use state and national standards as frameworks for intern design and assessment. These standards define the field's expectations for quality leadership readiness, are usually the basis for program content, and are strongly aligned to other national educational leadership standards that are often the basis for evaluating district leader practice. Thus, using these standards in internship assessment fosters coherence and supports an intern's ongoing professional learning in the program and beyond.

Throughout the internship, interns are expected to accumulate experiences across the leadership preparation standards, which they are to document in logs or other reporting mechanisms. They are also expected to complete various leadership-related tasks and projects, as is relevant to their district setting and their preparation program expectations. These tasks will likely include completed work that pertains to one or more nationally defined leadership preparation performance assessments (outlined below) and culminating preparation program projects, such as an action research project or capstone experience. The completed work may be compiled in an on-line portfolio, drop-box folder, or other information management system, as is commonly used among preparation programs for documentation and evaluation. The guidance provided below encompasses all such documentation and assessment completion, to support interns in their internship experiences and related assessment. Finally, reflection on the work and completed projects and assignments should be woven throughout the internship experience to foster increased knowledge and further skill development.

Candidate assessment in the internship occurs at four stages throughout the experience.

Stage 1: *Intern self-assessment and readiness*. The intern can use this initial assessment for determining skill needs and priorities and identifying projects and areas for performance-based work as a basis for planning in Stages 2 and 3. A primary way for interns to gain skills and demonstrate competency is by undertaking and completing performance assessment tasks, projects, or other complex assignments, that are aligned with standards and expectations for initial district leadership. This approach also includes review of standards and preparation program assessment requirements to be completed through the internship.

Stage 2: *Collaboration with district internship supervisor and preparation program advisor*. By meeting initially, the site supervisor, program advisor, and the intern can reach consensus and final approval of the internship plan, including means of documenting work and experiences and reporting results for projects or other completed tasks. Adjusting plans is expected and is a way to take advantage of new opportunities or address unforeseen problems that arise. Supervisors and advisors should guide and support appropriate changes to the initial internship plan.

Among the plans would be an outline of the projects, tasks, or work activities the intern would undertake to demonstrate performance in line with the NELP performance assessment expectations or other program-related performance demonstration requirements. The internship plan should also include procedures for documentation of all internship activities and their alignment to leadership standards and proficiencies.

Stage 3: *Monitoring progress in the implementation of the internship*. Monitoring will typically occur using logs and reflections and soliciting feedback from the district internship supervisor. Program advisors are encouraged to monitor the following throughout each intern's experience, using the intern's logs, reflections, and supervisory discussions:

♦ Leadership identity formation – how is the intern's understanding and identity with district leadership developing?
♦ Breadth of leadership skills and practices – does the intern have enough experiences in each standard?
♦ Depth of leadership experience – has the intern's leadership skills developed in depth in one or more standards areas? Has the intern achieved independence as a leader in one or more skill area?

They are also encouraged to monitor each intern's progress in completing any assigned projects or long-term tasks.

Stage 4: *Evaluation.* Program faculty will look across all the evidence that interns have provided to make a summative assessment about each candidate's readiness for program completion, recommendation for licensure or certification, and advancement to an initial district leader position. Program faculty should use a standards-based rubric to evaluate interns' report or portfolio of proficiencies and accomplishments and performance tasks, action research or other leadership projects. Where possible, each intern's portfolio and projects should be evaluated by two or more scorers, ideally independent of the program. Program faculty should also gather and review the following as part of evaluating an intern's performance:

♦ District internship supervisor feedback on the intern's performance and leadership readiness.
♦ Intern post-assessment and reflection of skills, dispositions, and leadership orientation.
♦ Logs or other documentation of work products completed, as aligned to the national or other standards.
♦ Leadership performance in relation to program, state, and national standards and program accreditation standards, if needed.
♦ State licensure assessment results (as may be relevant and available).

The Developmental Nature of the Internship

The internship is a multifaceted learning process in which interns integrate theory with practice by learning, practicing, performing, and reflecting on the craft of educational leadership. Through a series of leadership development experiences in an apprenticeship-like process, candidates develop leadership skills and a career orientation, assess their commitment to a career in the field, and receive feedback on their developing leadership knowledge, skills, dispositions, and performance.

The internship, while site specific, is typically designed in accordance with national and state school leadership standards and the guidelines for an internship: Interns demonstrate the ability to accept genuine responsibility for and enact leading, facilitating, and making decisions typical of those made by educational leaders. The experience(s) should provide interns with substantial responsibilities that increase over time in amount and complexity, as shown by the four levels below, and involve direct interaction and involvement with staff, students, parents, and community leaders.

Levels and Scope of Development for Interns

Level 1	Level 2	Level 3	Level 4
Observing	Participating	Initial Leading	Independent Leading
			Becoming more independent in leadership responsibilities
		Taking responsibility for leadership tasks, with oversight	
Being exposed to leadership work	Assisting and collaborating in leadership tasks		
10%–20% of internship	20%–30%	40%–50%	20%–30%

Level 1: Observing. At this initial level, interns' leadership development begins with job shadowing and exposure activities. This internship level begins the intern's organizational socialization, fostering role clarification, with exposure to school district functions and operations from a leader's perspective (Brody et al., 2010; Browne-Ferrigno, 2003). It also begins the intern's leadership identity development, shifting from school leader to district leader perspective (Browne-Ferrigno, 2003; Crow, 2012). Internship activities at this level might be observing by shadowing a superintendent or assistant superintendent for a day or week, attending leadership team meetings and committee meetings as an observer, and exploring the district's community to learn more about its context. Interns can also visit various non-academic departments, services, and operations (such as the central office functions, transportation, maintenance, food services, and support services) to observe work first-hand, interview supervisors and staff about their responsibilities, and learn how all district systems are connected and coordinated. This initial level, of only observing, should be brief (no more than 10%–20% of the whole experience), but some leadership exposure activities – such as attending leadership team meetings – could be incorporated throughout the internship, particularly as these activities may be germane to other work.

Level 2: Participating. At the second level, interns would begin to participate in leadership work, assisting other district leaders in supervision and management. The intern is exposed to how to perform an array of leadership tasks by working alongside his or her supervisor or mentor. This level is termed as learning through peripheral participation (Lave & Wenger, 1991). The learning process in this level entails both doing and observing, in which interns co-participate with their district supervisors in completing part of a leadership task while simultaneously observing how their district supervisors perform the work (Williams et al., 2004). At this level, interns are also simultaneously able to work with different district constituencies – principals, teachers, other staff, parents, and community members – gaining insight into leadership responsibilities and perspectives. This level, while longer than the first, should be transitional, leading to more independent leadership work in the next two levels, and should be about 20%–30% of the internship experience.

Level 3: Initial leading. At the third level, interns begin to take independent responsibility for portions of leadership work, while being closely guided and supervised. Darling-Hammond et al. (2007) describe this type of internship experience as hands-on, on-site experience under the guidance of an experienced practitioner … to gain knowledge and skills they will need to address the challenges of the position. This is the longest phase, about 40%–50% of the internship, during which interns have opportunities to conduct leadership work across core domains of responsibility, such as those defined by national standards (National Policy Board for Educational Administration, 2015), while being closely supervised by his or her district leader or internship supervisor. Interns' work resembles on-the-job training, in which interns develop skills through real work experience. During this phase, interns are coached in how to perform their leadership work and encouraged to make connections to coursework, while deepening their leadership identity and skills (Shoho et al., 2012). Interns will likely begin their internship projects or tasks to be completed as demonstration of their performance and for inclusion in their portfolio or other assessment system.

Level 4: Independent leading. At this fourth level, interns take even more independent responsibility for leadership work, with little guidance and supervision. At this level, interns are primarily mentored, rather than coached, to reinforce and deepen their leadership skills (Crow, 2012). Interns are likely to work independently on discrete projects or problems of practice, gaining depth in their experience, rather than striving for breadth across areas of work. This work moves the intern from the level of peripheral participation to central participation, enacting district leader work as would be more typical for a beginning leader. This work is likely to occur during the latter part of the intern's experience and allows him/her to demonstrate new acquired leadership skills and practices and will likely yield accomplishments that can serve as exemplars of skill proficiency when pursuing new positions. Interns will complete their performance assessment tasks and projects, and any other culminating assignment, like an action research project or capstone. This level is likely to be about 20%–30% of the intern's experience.

Meeting Professional Standards

Leadership preparation candidates must be familiar with two sets of educational leadership standards. First are the National Standards for Leadership Preparation (NELP) which guide superintendent preparation programs and the second are the Professional Standards for Educational Leaders (PSEL) which set policy for the evaluation of practicing school administrators. Both sets of standards were developed and adopted by the National Policy Board for Educational Administration. The Board is made up of the following professional organizations:

American Association of School Administrators (AASA)
Council of Chief State School Officers (CCSSO)
International Council of Professors of Educational Leadership (ICPEL)

National Association of Elementary School Principals (NAESP)
National Association of Secondary School Principals (NASSP)
University Council for Educational Administration (UCEA)

A crosswalk between these two sets of standards is presented in Appendix A.3.

The PSEL standards were designed to identify and establish a set of common professional standards for school leaders. It was felt that a set of common standards would provide an avenue for improvement efforts in a variety of areas of administrative leadership. The PSEL sets high benchmarks for the educational leader to meet (National Policy Board for Educational Administration, 2015). The ten standards include:

1. Create a mission, vision, and core values.
2. Act with ethics and professional norms.
3. Strive for equity and cultural responsiveness.
4. Develop intellectually rigorous curriculum, instruction, and assessment.
5. Cultivate a community of care and support for students.
6. Develop the professional capacity of school personnel.
7. Foster a professional community for teachers and staff.
8. Engage families and community.
9. Manage operations and management.
10. Support continuous school improvement.

Many are standards that can only be fully mastered through full-time leadership positions. The internship, however, will be the beginning experience for approaching these standards.

The second set of national educational leadership standards (NELP) are for the preparation of aspiring leaders. Leadership preparation programs that want or are required to be nationally accredited must align their program content and internships to the national educational leadership preparation standards (National Policy Board for Educational Administration, 2018).

The eight standards include:

1. Lead, design, and implement a district vision and mission.
2. Advocate for ethical decisions and cultivate professional norms and culture.
3. Develop and maintain a supportive, equitable, culturally responsive, and inclusive district culture.
4. Evaluate, design, cultivate, and implement coherent systems of curriculum, instruction, data systems, supports, assessment, and instructional leadership.
5. Understand and engage families and communities and advocate for district, student, and community needs.
6. Develop, monitor, evaluate, and manage data-informed and equitable district systems for operations, resources, technology, and human capital management.
7. Cultivate relationships, lead collaborative decision making and governance, and represent and advocate for district needs in broader policy conversations.
8. Candidates successfully complete an internship under the supervision of knowledgeable, expert practitioners that engages candidates in multiple and diverse district settings and provides candidates with coherent, authentic, and sustained opportunities to synthesize and apply the knowledge and skills identified in NELP

Standards 1–7 in ways that approximate the full range of responsibilities required of district-level leaders and enable them to promote the current and future success and well-being of each student and adult in their district.

- Candidates are provided a variety of coherent, authentic, field, or clinical internship experiences within multiple district environments that afford opportunities to interact with stakeholders and synthesize and apply the content knowledge and develop and refine the professional skills articulated in each of the components included in NELP district-level program standards 1–7.
- Candidates are provided a minimum of six months of concentrated (10–15 hours per week) internship or clinical experiences that include authentic leadership activities within a district setting.
- Candidates are provided a supervisor who has demonstrated effectiveness as an educational leader within a district setting; understands the specific district context; is present for a significant portion of the internship; is selected collaboratively by the intern, a representative of the district, and program faculty; and is provided with training by the supervising institution.

Interns should be aware of these program standards and review them with their program faculty to learn about their programs' approach to meeting these standards and how this approach and use of the standards would shape their internship opportunities and expectations.

In addition to these national standards, the intern should also be knowledgeable of the differing local, state, and national professional associations that provide the guidance and resources for effective school leadership. Although supportive of the NPBEA standards, each association may offer additional standards, competencies, proficiencies, and other resources to assist school leaders in a particular field. It is strongly recommended that the intern become an active member in the professional associations of their choice for continued and further professional development, networking, and mentoring opportunities.

As well, the intern should review their respective state standards to ensure that the intern plan activities meet these requirements also. Keep in mind that most state licensure exams or assessments are based on state standards rather than national standards, although most overlap and the similarities are much greater than any differences. Typically, state standards address all the national standards and either add additional ones or elaborate on some details of a standard. States differ in how they assess readiness based on their standards – some have exams and others require performance assessments or portfolios.

References

Bennis, W. (2003). *On becoming a leader* (revised ed.). Cambridge, MA: Perseus Publishing.

Brody, J. L., Vissa, J., & Weathers, J. M. (2010). School leader professional socialization: The contribution of focused observation. *Journal of Research on Leadership Education*, 5(14), 611–651.

Browne-Ferrigno, T. (2003). Becoming a principal: Role conception, initial socialization, role-identity transformation, purposeful engagement. *Educational Administration Quarterly*, 39(4), 468–503.

Crow, G. M. (2012). A critical-constructivist perspective on mentoring and coaching for leadership. In S. J. Fletcher & C. A. Mullin (Eds.), *Sage handbook on mentoring and coaching in education*. Thousand Oaks, CA: Sage Publications.

Darling-Hammond, L., LaPointe, M., Meyerson, D., Orr. M. T., & Cohen, C. (2007). *Preparing school leaders for a changing world: Lessons from exemplary leadership development programs*. Stanford, CA: Stanford University, Stanford Educational Leadership Institute. Retrieved from https://edpolicy.stanford.edu/sites/default/files/publications/preparing-school-leaders-changing-world-lessons-exemplary-leadership-development-programs_1.pdf

Lave, L., & Wenger, E. (1991). *Situated learning: Legitimate peripheral participation*. Cambridge: Cambridge University Press.

Leithwood, K., Louis, K. S., Anderson, S., & Wahlstrom, K. (2004). *How leadership influences student learning*. New York, NY: Wallace Foundation. Retrieved from https://www.wallacefoundation.org/knowledge-center/Documents/How-Leadership-Influences-Student-Learning.pdf

National Policy Board for Educational Administration. (2015). *Professional standards for educational leaders 2015*. Reston, VA: Author. Retrieved from http://www.npbea.org/wp-content/uploads/2017/06/Professional-Standards-for-Educational-Leaders_2015.pdf

Scott, D. (2017). Education Commission of the States. *2017 State Policy Review: School and District Leadership*. Retrieved from www.ecs.org

Shoho, A., Barnett, B. G., & Martinez, P. (2012). Enhancing "OJT" internships with interactive coaching. *Planning & Changing*, 43(1–2), 161–182.

Williams, E. J., Matthews, J., & Baugh, S. (2004). Developing a mentoring internship model for school leadership: Using legitimate peripheral participation. *Mentoring & Tutoring: Partnership in Learning*, 12(1), 53–57.

Internship Assessment

The first step in developing the internship plan is to assess your current strengths and weaknesses (areas for needed growth in knowledge and skill) regarding expectations from the program, state and national standards, and other personal areas for leadership growth and development. This includes becoming fully aware of one's dispositions for leadership. As each intern begins to plan for growth in needed knowledge and skill through the internship experience, it is imperative to consider the goals and needs of the school in which you will be serving. Thus, the initial internship plan should include goals and activities for personal leadership development and school improvement. This is the responsibility and opportunity for each intern to add to generic guidelines for an internship experience with the unique needs of the intern and school district.

In this stage of plan development, the intern must gather and analyze various personal and school documents. These include the NELP Standards self-assessment, dispositions assessment, school improvement and/or strategic plans, and NELP performance assessments. The following sections further explain the needed documentation. The final section provides guidelines for analysis and reporting.

1.1 NELP Standards for District-Level Leaders Self-Assessment

The standards set by the National Policy Board for Educational Administration (NPBEA, 2018) include seven NELP standards that aspiring school leaders are expected to master as they begin to lead their districts. Although complete mastery may only come from extended experience in the position, interns are expected to be cognizant of these professional standards and use them as goals for continuous development. Complete the pre-self-assessment as accurately and honestly as possible and note the standards in greatest need for focus in the internship plan. Discuss the findings with your district supervisor and/or program advisor. This self-assessment will be taken at the end of the internship for comparative purposes. Reflections and documentation of progress toward all standards will be required in the final professional report at the end of the internship. All items on the self-assessment are skills you are expected to possess.

DOI: 10.4324/9781003299493-2

Pre- and Post-Internship NELP Self-Assessment

Your choices for each item are:

HD (high degree) – This indicates you have significant experiences concerning this topic and additional experience is not needed

SD (some degree) – This indicates you have some experiences concerning this topic, but additional experience is needed.

LD (low degree) – This indicates you have little or a few experiences concerning this topic and significantly more experience is needed.

NONE – This indicates you have no experience concerning this topic and experience is needed.

NELP Standard 1

Vision, Mission, and Improvement

NELP Standard Component 1.1

Program completers understand and demonstrate the capacity to collaboratively design, communicate, and evaluate a district mission and vision that reflects a core set of values and priorities that include data use, technology, values, equity, diversity, digital citizenship, and community.

Evaluate existing mission and vision processes and statements	HD SD LD None
Collaboratively design an actionable district mission and vision attentive to such considerations as data use, technology, values, equity, diversity, digital citizenship, and community	HD SD LD None
Develop a comprehensive plan for communicating the mission and vision to multiple constituencies	HD SD LD None

NELP Standard Component 1.2

Program completers understand and demonstrate the capacity to lead district strategic planning and continuous improvement processes that engage diverse stakeholders in data collection, diagnosis, design, implementation, and evaluation.

Evaluate existing improvement processes	HD SD LD None
Develop a district-wide improvement process that includes data collection, diagnosis, design, implementation, and evaluation	HD SD LD None
Articulate a process for strategic planning	HD SD LD None
Develop an implementation plan to support the improvement process	HD SD LD None

NELP Standard 2

Ethics and Professional Norms

NELP Standard Component 2.1

Program completers understand and demonstrate the capacity to reflect on, communicate about, and cultivate professional dispositions and norms (i.e., fairness, integrity, transparency, trust, collaboration, perseverance, reflection, lifelong learning, and digital citizenship) and professional district and school cultures.

Engage in reflective practice	HD SD LD None
Cultivate professional norms among diverse constituencies	HD SD LD None
Model and communicate professional norms (i.e., integrity, fairness, transparency, trust, equity, democracy, digital citizenship, diversity, inclusiveness, and the belief that each child can learn)	HD SD LD None
Use professional norms as a basis for building organizational culture	HD SD LD None

NELP Standard Component 2.2

Program completers understand and demonstrate the capacity to evaluate and advocate for ethical and legal decisions.

Evaluate ethical dimensions of complex issues, including stewardship and use of district resources	HD SD LD None
Analyze decisions in terms of established ethical frameworks	HD SD LD None
Advocate for ethical decisions	HD SD LD None

NELP Standard Component 2.3

Program completers understand and demonstrate the capacity to model ethical behavior in their personal conduct and relationships and to cultivate ethical behavior in others.

Model ethical behavior in their personal conduct and relationships with others	HD SD LD None
Cultivate ethical behavior in others	HD SD LD None

NELP Standard 3

Inclusiveness and Cultural Responsiveness

NELP Standard Component 3.1

Program completers understand and demonstrate the capacity to evaluate, cultivate, and advocate for a supportive and inclusive district culture.

Evaluate district culture	HD SD LD None
Use research and evidence to design and cultivate a supportive and inclusive district culture	HD SD LD None
Advocate for a supportive and inclusive district culture	HD SD LD None

NELP Standard Component 3.2

Program completers understand and demonstrate the capacity to evaluate, cultivate, and advocate for equitable access to safe and nurturing schools and the opportunities and resources, including instructional materials, technologies, classrooms, teachers, interventions, and adult relationships, necessary to support the success and well-being of each student.

Evaluate sources of inequality and bias in the allocation of educational opportunities and resources, including instructional, materials technologies, classrooms, teachers, interventions, and adult relationships	HD SD LD None
Cultivate the equitable use of educational resources and opportunities through procedures, guidelines, norms, and values	HD SD LD None
Advocate for equitable access to educational resources, procedures, and opportunities	HD SD LD None

NELP Standard Component 3.3

Program completers understand and demonstrate the capacity to evaluate, advocate, and cultivate equitable, inclusive, and culturally responsive instructional and behavioral support practices among teachers and staff.

Evaluate root causes of inequity and bias	HD SD LD None
Develop district policies or procedures that cultivate equitable, inclusive, and culturally responsive practice among teachers and staff	HD SD LD None
Advocate for culturally responsive instructional and behavior support practices among district staff and across district schools	HD SD LD None
Cultivate culturally responsive instructional and behavior support practices across the district and its schools	HD SD LD None

NELP Standard 4

Learning and Instruction

NELP Standard Component 4.1

Program completers understand and can demonstrate the capacity to evaluate, design, and implement high-quality curricula, the use of technology, and other services and supports for academic and non-academic student programs.

Evaluate (a) curricula, use of technology, and other supports (b) academic and non-academic systems, and (c) coordination among systems and supports	HD SD LD None
Use research and evidence to propose designs and implementation strategies for improving coordination and coherence among (a) curricula, instructional technologies, and other supports, and (b) academic and non-academic systems	HD SD LD None

NELP Standard Component 4.2

Program completers understand and can demonstrate the capacity to collaboratively evaluate, design, and cultivate systems of support, coaching, and professional development for educators, educational professionals, and school and district leaders, including themselves, that promote reflection, digital literacy, distributed leadership, data literacy, equity, improvement, and student success.

Use research and data to evaluate the coordination, coherence, and relevance of the district's systems of support, coaching, and professional development for educators, educational professionals, and leaders	HD SD LD None
Use research to propose designs and implementation strategies for cultivating systems of support and professional development that promote reflection, digital literacy, distributed leadership, data literacy, equity, improvement, and student success	HD SD LD None

NELP Standard Component 4.3

Program completers understand and can demonstrate the capacity to design, implement, and evaluate a developmentally appropriate, accessible, and culturally responsive system of assessments and data collection.

Evaluate the quality of formative and summative assessments of student learning	HD SD LD None
Evaluate coordination and coherence among academic and non-academic assessments and use data from these sources to support instructional improvement, student learning and well-being, and instructional leadership	HD SD LD None
Use research to propose designs and implementation strategies for district-wide assessment systems that are culturally responsive and accessible	HD SD LD None

NELP Standard Component 4.4

Program completers understand and demonstrate the capacity to design, implement, and evaluate district-wide use of coherent systems of curriculum, instruction, assessment, student services, technology, and instructional resources that support the needs of each student in the district.

Engage appropriate staff in gathering, synthesizing, and using data   HD SD LD None
   to evaluate the quality, coordination, and coherence in and
   among the district's academic and non-academic services

Use research to propose designs and implementation strategies   HD SD LD None
   for improving coordination and coherence among the district's
   academic and non-academic systems

Use technology and performance management systems to monitor,   HD SD LD None
   analyze, and evaluate district curriculum, instruction, services,
   assessment practices, and results

NELP Standard 5

Community and External Leadership

NELP Standard Component 5.1

Program completers understand and demonstrate the capacity to represent and support district schools in engaging diverse families in strengthening student learning in and out of school.

Represent the district and its schools	HD SD LD None
Support the efforts of district schools in engaging diverse families in strengthening student learning in and out of school	HD SD LD None
Make decisions about when and how to engage families	HD SD LD None

NELP Standard Component 5.2

Program completers understand and demonstrate the capacity to understand, engage, and effectively collaborate and communicate with, through oral, written, and digital means, diverse families, community members, partners, and other constituencies to benefit learners, schools, and the district as a whole.

Develop systems and processes designed to support district personnel's understanding of diverse families, community members, partners, and other constituencies	HD SD LD None
Collaborate with diverse community members, partners, and other constituencies	HD SD LD None
Foster regular, two-way communication with community members partners, and other constituencies	HD SD LD None
Develop communication for oral, written, and digital distribution distribution targeted to a diverse stakeholder community	HD SD LD None
Engage community members, partners, and other constituents in district efforts	HD SD LD None

NELP Standard Component 5.3

Program completers understand and demonstrate the capacity to communicate through oral, written, and digital means within the larger organizational, community, and political contexts and cultivate relationships with members of the business, civic, and policy community in support of their advocacy for district, school, student, and community needs.

Conduct a needs assessment of the district, school, students, and community	HD SD LD None
Develop a plan for accessing resources that addresses district needs	HD SD LD None
Cultivate collaborative relationships with district constituencies	HD SD LD None
Develop oral, written, and digital communications targeted on the larger organizational, community, and political contexts	HD SD LD None
Advocate for district and community needs	HD SD LD None

Standard 6

Operations and Management

NELP Standard Component 6.1

Program completers understand and demonstrate the capacity to develop, communicate, implement, and evaluate data-informed and equitable management, communication, technology, governance, and operation systems at the district level to support schools in realizing the district's mission and vision.

Evaluate management and operation systems	HD SD LD None
Use data and research to propose designs for improving the coordination and impact of district management, communication, technology, governance, and operation of systems	HD SD LD None
Communicate with relevant stakeholders about the relationship between the district's management, operation, and governance systems and the district's mission and vision	HD SD LD None
Develop an implementation plan to support improved district systems	HD SD LD None

NELP Standard Component 6.2

Program completers understand and demonstrate the capacity to develop, communicate, implement, and evaluate a data-based district resourcing plan and support schools in developing their school-level resourcing plans.

Use data to evaluate district resource needs and practices	HD SD LD None
Use research and data to design an equitable district resourcing plan and support schools in designing school resourcing plans that coordinate resources with needs	HD SD LD None
Communicate about district resources needs and plans	HD SD LD None
Develop an implementation plan for the district's resourcing plan	HD SD LD None

NELP Standard Component 6.3

Program completers understand and demonstrate the capacity to develop, implement, and evaluate coordinated, data-informed systems for hiring, retaining, supervising, and developing school and district staff to support the district's collective instructional and leadership capacity.

Use data to evaluate district human resources needs	HD SD LD None
Use research and data to develop a district-level system for hiring retention, development, and supervision of school/district personnel	HD SD LD None
Evaluate candidates' materials for instructional and leadership positions	HD SD LD None
Implement systems of leadership supervision, evaluation, feedback, and support	HD SD LD None

Standard 7

Policy, Governance, and Advocacy

NELP Standard Component 7.1

Program completers understand and demonstrate the capacity to represent the district, advocate for district needs, and cultivate a respectful and responsive relationship with the district's board of education focused on achieving the shared mission and vision of the district.

Represent the district and its mission, strengths, and needs to the board of education	HD	SD	LD	None
Cultivate a positive, respectful, and responsive relationship with the board	HD	SD	LD	None
Advocate for board actions that will support the mission and vision of the district and meet district needs	HD	SD	LD	None

NELP Standard Component 7.2

Program completers understand and demonstrate the capacity to design, implement, cultivate, and evaluate effective and collaborative systems for district governance that engage multiple and diverse stakeholder groups, including school and district personnel, families, community stakeholders, and board members.

Evaluate district governance and stakeholder engagement systems	HD	SD	LD	None
Design governance systems that engage multiple and diverse stakeholder groups	HD	SD	LD	None
Implement strategies (i.e., communication) that supports stakeholder engagement in district governance	HD	SD	LD	None
Cultivate and coordinate an effective and collaborative system for district governance	HD	SD	LD	None

NELP Standard Component 7.3

Program completers understand and demonstrate the capacity to evaluate, engage in decision-making, implement, and appropriately communicate about district, state, and national policies, laws, rules, and regulations.

Evaluate the implications of educational policy for district practices	HD	SD	LD	None
Develop a plan for the implementation of laws, rights, policies, and regulations	HD	SD	LD	None
Communicate about district, state, and national policies, laws, rules, and regulations	HD	SD	LD	None
Coordinate decisions and district policies with policies and/or regulations from local, state, and federal policy entities	HD	SD	LD	None

NELP Standard Component 7.4

Program completers understand the implications of larger cultural, social, economic, legal, and political interests, changes, and expectations and demonstrate the capacity to evaluate and represent district needs and priorities within larger policy conversations and advocate for district needs and priorities at the local, state, and national levels.

Use evidence to evaluate district needs and priorities such as education policy conversations and emerging challenges (i.e., ransomware)	HD SD LD None
Represent the district and its priorities and needs at the local, state, and national levels	HD SD LD None
Advocate for the needs and priorities of the district at the local, state, and national levels	HD SD LD None

Note: Save a copy of your pre-assessment. At the end of the internship, circle your choices with a different color of ink. Compare this second self-assessment to your initial self-assessment. Where was your growth and development greatest? What evidence do you have to support this?

Using your post self-assessment ratings, identify areas for further professional development.

1.2 Dispositions Self-Assessment

A critical part of each candidate's fieldwork is the development of effective dispositions and interpersonal skills. According to Merriam-Webster online dictionary, a disposition is a tendency to think or act in a particular way. Leadership experts agree that selected dispositions are critical for effective leadership practice, and that leadership knowledge and skills are insufficient without these (Bryk, Sebring, Allensworth, Luppescu, & Easton, 2010; Louis, Leithwood, Wahlstrom, & Anderson, 2010). Hackett and Hortman (2008) argue that dispositions motivate the application of knowledge and skills. In recent years, a variety of dispositions have been highlighted as critical for effective leadership practice, particularly those related to ethics, caring, social justice, and change oriented dispositions (Brown, 2006; Gerstl-Pepin, Killeen, & Hasazi, 2006; Theoharis, 2007; Wagner et al., 2006).

It is important for district leaders to be cognizant of their dispositions and to be able to identify the dispositions of other leaders in the school district (Oswald-Herold et al., 2018). Understanding the specific traits and dispositions of school leaders will help the superintendent identify the most appropriate individuals to lead campuses. Leadership of campuses, departments, and programs is key to having a positive effect on staff, students, and community (Johnston, Wilson, & Almerico, 2018). Several leadership preparation programs have adopted an experiential and reflective learning approach to developing leadership candidates' dispositions, organized around those most essential to effective leadership practices (Creasap et al., 2005; McKenzie et al., 2006; Rucinski & Bauch, 2006). Thus, there appears to be conditions under which leadership dispositions can be developed – when they can be defined and assessed to set learning goals and measure progress and when interns use reflective practices to question existing assumptions and consider and try out alternatives (Creasap et al., 2005; Osterman & Kottkamp, 2004).

According to Osterman and Kottkamp (2004), reflective practice is an effective means of experiential learning for leadership development. It enables leadership candidates to develop an awareness of their habitual actions and assumptions and consider their effectiveness relative to intentions. Learning through reflective practice is guided by Kolb's four learning stages – having (1) concrete experiences; (2) analyzing and questioning one's assumptions and actions in these experiences; (3) considering alternatives through reconceptualization; and (4) active experimentation with new actions and approaches (Kolb, 1984). This cycle can be formalized in a learning plan to guide candidates' learning. Drawing from their own experiences and a program's priority dispositions, candidates can analyze and reflect upon their dispositions – both actions and assumptions and consider alternative approaches.

Once identified, a candidate can create a disposition-related learning plan linked to the learning activities that they might use to try out new actions and assumptions. Specific, focused assignments can enable candidates to develop specific dispositions. Structuring learning experiences as part of the active experimentation phase can promote learning. Brown, for example, found that by participating in assignments requiring the examination of assumptions, values and beliefs, and competing worldviews, leadership candidates can transform their dispositions around social justice and equity (Brown, 2006).

Candidates begin with a self-assessment to select a disposition or interpersonal skill to strengthen or improve. They then discuss their selection with the advisor for feedback and strategy. The candidate and advisor decide on a relevant short-term goal, the evidence of progress toward it, and strategies for skill acquisition and mastery through the internship or other experiences. Finally, the candidate and advisor decide how progress is to be documented and how to use journal reflections to support skill/disposition development over the internship.

For example, using this approach, one intern wanted to improve her ability to speak up and take initiative in small group committee meetings. She measured her frequency as a baseline and set a personal goal to increase the frequency of her initiative taking and contributing to group discussions. She informed her committee colleagues about her goal and solicited their feedback on her progress, as well as logged her own efforts. Over time, she increased the frequency and at the same time became more comfortable with taking initiative and actively contributing to small group meetings.

As a preparatory exercise, we strongly recommend that interns engage in a leadership disposition self-assessment. It is important to know and understand your educational leadership dispositions. Gaining insight into your dispositional strengths and areas for improvement comes from self-assessment and feedback from peers and others. Thus, it is recommended that you complete one copy of the evaluation yourself and then ask your school supervisor to complete the assessment for you as well. Then, compare the results of your self-assessment with the assessments made by others. You can then use your results to assist in the development of your internship plan.

Dispositions Assessment

Please circle the indicator that you believe most accurately describes evidence of the following dispositions. This is not a recommendation form on the merit or expertise of the person, but an assessment of your perspective of the beliefs behind the words and/or actions of the person. Please complete this assessment as accurately and honestly as possible. Thank you for your time and effort.

SE (strong evidence); LE (limited evidence); NS (not seen); OE (opposing evidence)

The intern believes in, values, and is committed to:

1. The educability of all	SE	LE	NS	OE
2. A school vision of high standards of learning	SE	LE	NS	OE
3. Continuous school improvement	SE	LE	NS	OE
4. The inclusion of all members of the school community	SE	LE	NS	OE
5. Ensuring that students have the knowledge, skills, and values needed to become successful adults	SE	LE	NS	OE
6. A willingness to continuously examine one's own assumptions, beliefs, and practices	SE	LE	NS	OE
7. Doing the work required for high levels of personal and organizational performance	SE	LE	NS	OE
8. Student learning as a fundamental purpose of schooling	SE	LE	NS	OE
9. The proposition that all students can learn	SE	LE	NS	OE
10. The variety of ways in which students can learn	SE	LE	NS	OE
11. Lifelong learning for self and others	SE	LE	NS	OE
12. Professional development as an integral part of school improvement	SE	LE	NS	OE
13. Benefits that diversity brings to the school community	SE	LE	NS	OE
14. A safe and supportive learning environment	SE	LE	NS	OE
15. Preparing students to contribute to society	SE	LE	NS	OE
16. Making management decisions to enhance learning and teaching	SE	LE	NS	OE
17. Taking risks to improve schools	SE	LE	NS	OE
18. Trusting people and their judgments	SE	LE	NS	OE
19. Accepting responsibility	SE	LE	NS	OE
20. High-quality standards, expectations, and performances	SE	LE	NS	OE
21. Involving stakeholders in management processes	SE	LE	NS	OE
22. A safe environment	SE	LE	NS	OE
23. School operating as an integral part of the community	SE	LE	NS	OE
24. Collaboration and communication with families	SE	LE	NS	OE
25. Involve families and other stakeholders in school decision-making processes	SE	LE	NS	OE
26. The proposition that diversity enriches the school	SE	LE	NS	OE
27. Families as partners in the education of their children	SE	LE	NS	OE
28. The proposition that families have the best interests of their children in mind	SE	LE	NS	OE
29. Resources of the family and community needing to be brought to bear on the education of students	SE	LE	NS	OE
30. The right of every student to a free, quality education	SE	LE	NS	OE
31. Bring ethical principles to the decision-making process	SE	LE	NS	OE
32. Subordinating one's own interest to the good of the school community	SE	LE	NS	OE
33. Accepting consequences for one's principles and actions	SE	LE	NS	OE
34. Using the influence of one's office constructively in the service of all students and their families	SE	LE	NS	OE
35. Development of a caring school community	SE	LE	NS	OE

36. Education as a key to opportunity and social mobility	SE	LE	NS	OE
37. Recognizing a variety of ideas, values, and cultures	SE	LE	NS	OE
38. Using legal systems to protect student rights and improve student opportunities	SE	LE	NS	OE

1.3 School District Assessment

It is imperative that interns fully know and understand the *state of affairs* of the organization with a districtwide perspective. Although most interns will conduct their internship in the district where they are employed, this does not guarantee an adequate background for district-level leadership. Superintendents must deal with numerous and very different issues and concerns from those experienced by building-level leaders. Prior to conducting internship activities where you will be observed by program and site supervisors, as well as administrators, teachers, and staff, the intern must gain the needed, relevant information about the school district. These can be gathered from current documents such as:

- District needs assessments
- Strategic or action plans
- Vision and mission statements
- Recent state, regional, and/or national accreditation reports
- District improvement plans

One could assume that the first four bullets above lead to the district improvement plan. Having an improvement plan, however, is not enough – strategies and who will be responsible for change is a critical component of district improvement (Stevenson, 2019). As you review the various district documents, look for evidence of what actions the district plans to take and the responsible parties.

Interns must also be fully knowledgeable and aware of other crucial aspects of the district. This would include demographics, fiscal and facility status, district history and traditions, and current board and community relations. It is strongly recommended that interns meet with the site supervisor to discuss these aspects of the district and especially cover any current pressing or sensitive board and/or community political issues or concerns.

1.4 NELP Performance Assessments

Demonstrating Experience and Proficiency across Standards

In preparation for the internship, the intern should know how standards-based evidence will be collected, as part of meeting program internship standards (NELP standard 8). This will likely include a listing of the major areas of significant knowledge and experience, as well as the major areas of limited knowledge and experience. The intern is advised to begin collecting documentation of evidence supporting strengths and performance that meet each standard. Evidence collected at the present time should be included. This can be done through logs or other internship tracking mechanisms, as well as online information management systems or portfolios.

In addition, a primary means for interns to gain skills and demonstrate competency is by undertaking and completing performance assessment tasks, projects, or other complex assignments, that are aligned with standards and expectations for school district leadership.

These can include but are not necessarily limited to four primary performance assessment tasks that NELP requires be completed as part of leadership preparation. These four assessment requirements are outlined below as an exemplar for internship planning to ensure breadth and depth of experiences and skill development. They can also be used to identify key projects or tasks for interns to undertake and the means of evaluating skill accomplishments.

NELP Performance Assessment Standards and Requirements

NELP requires that leadership candidates demonstrate leadership proficiency through completion of four performance-based assessments. While these may be completed through course-based assignments, they are more likely to be completed as part of the internship, because of the field-based practice opportunities. Interns should be aware of these four performance assessments, program expectations for their completion, reporting and scoring, and their alignment to and support from local district priorities. Throughout Stage 3 are a series of initial, substantive projects or tasks that align with these assessment expectations and can be used to meet these performance assessment requirements, unless other program-specific ones are required.

University and other preparation programs that are "nationally recognized" or seeking national recognition must submit reports to NELP assessing the skill level on the following four performance assessment requirements and the NELP standards most closely aligned.

Assessment 3: This assessment area encompasses the competencies and skills of leading a school's instructional core in curriculum, instruction, assessment, and the structures and supports for enhanced student learning. The demonstration of the candidate's leadership and management skills within a field-based setting, corresponding to NELP standards 1, 2, 3, and 6, is the basis for this assessment area.

Assessment 4: This assessment area encompasses all areas of school leadership but can be focused primarily on vision and priority setting, adherence to ethical principles and professional norms, developing an equitable and inclusive culture, and managing resources, systems, policies, and practices in supporting student learning. Demonstration of candidate's leadership and management skills within a field-based setting, corresponding to NELP standards 1, 2, 3, and 6.

Assessment 5: This performance assessment area corresponds most to the overall aim of the NELP standards, which is to promote the current and future success and well-being of each student and adult. To that end, this assessment area requires interns to demonstrate their knowledge and skills in supporting and promoting student learning through an equitable, responsive, and inclusive school culture and effective, coherent system of curriculum, instruction, assessments, and supports. Such demonstration is intended to link the intern's work, such as through a project or task, to how it supports and effective student learning environment. Demonstration of candidate's leadership skills in supporting an effective P-12 student learning environment, corresponding to NELP standards 3–4.

Assessment 6: This performance assessment area corresponds most closely to how the intern works to engage families and the community to support student learning and school improvement generally, as well as communicate about and advocate on behalf of the school's and community's needs. Demonstration of candidate's leadership skills in the areas of family and community relations, corresponding to NELP standard 5.

In completing these performance assessment tasks, interns must provide evidence, either through documentation, reports, or supervisor feedback of their proficiency and accomplishments, with consideration for the strength and quality of the evidence. This includes clearly showing alignment to standards, defining the knowledge and skills used, evidence of capacity to develop, evaluate, and apply these, and evidence of mastery for corresponding components and standards. NELP defines three performance levels to be used in evaluating assessments. These include:

Level 1 – Approaching. At this level, the intern has developed some knowledge and understanding or meets some but not all component expectations, but not sufficiently to practice all component expectations independently.

Level 2 – Meets. At this performance level, the intern has developed knowledge and understanding and demonstrates the capacity to meet all component expectations, at an acceptable level for an initial school leader and is ready for independent school leadership.

Level 3 – Exceeds. At this performance level, the intern exceeds expectations by demonstrating the knowledge, understanding and skills to meet all component expectations, as an effective school leader and is ready for independent initial school leadership.

References

Brown, K. M. (2006). Leadership for social justice and equity: Evaluating a transformative framework and andragogy. *Educational Administration Quarterly*, 42, 700–745.

Bryk, A. S., Sebring, P. B., Allensworth, E., Luppescu, S., & Easton, J. Q. (2010). *Organizing schools for improvement: Lessons from Chicago*. Chicago: University of Chicago Press.

Creasap, S. A., Peters, A. L., & Uline, C. L. (2005). The effects of guided reflection on educational leadership practice: Mentoring and portfolio writing as a means to transformative learning for early career principals. *Journal of School Leadership*, 15(4), 352–386.

Gerstl-Pepin, C., Killeen, K., & Hasazi, S. (2006). Utilizing an "ethic of care" in leadership preparation. *Journal of Educational Administration*, 44(3), 250. Retrieved from: http://proquest.umi.com/pqdweb?did=1127945551&Fmt=7&clientId=15403&RQT=309&VName=PQD

Hackett, P. T., & Hortman, J. W. (2008). The relationship of emotional competencies to transformational leadership: Using a corporate model to assess the dispositions of educational leaders. *Journal of Educational Research & Policy Studies*, 8(1), 92–111.

Johnston, P., Wilson, A., & Almerico, G.M. (2018). Meeting psychometric requirements for disposition assessment: Valid and reliable indicators of teacher dispositions. *Journal of Instructional Pedagogies*, 21. Retrieved from: https://files.eric.ed.gov/fulltext/EJ1194249.pdf

Kolb, D. A. (1984). Experiential learning: Experience as the source of learning and development. New Jersey: Prentice-Hall.

Louis, K. S., Leithwood, K., Wahlstrom, K. L., & Anderson, S. E. (2010). *Investigating the links to improved student learning. Final report of research findings*. New York, NY: Wallace Foundation.

McKenzie, K. B., Skrla, L., & Scheurich, J. J. (2006). Preparing instructional leadership for social justice. *Journal of School Leadership*, 16, 158–170.

National Policy Board for Educational Administration NPBEA. (2018). National Educational Leadership Preparation (NELP) Program Standards - Building Level. Reston, VA: Author. Retrieved from: http://www.npbea.org/wp-content/uploads/2018/11/NELP-Building-Standards.pdf

Osterman, K. F., & Kottkamp, R. B. (2004). *Reflective practice for educators* (2nd ed.). Thousand Oaks, CA: Corwin Press.

Oswald-Herold, C., Elbert, N., & Feit, M.E. (2018). *Foundational & emerging models of leadership development: A review of the literature and a taxonomy of leadership development programs,* 10–11. Retrieved from: https://501commons.org/learn/research/foundational-emerging-models-of-leadership-development

Rucinski, D. A., & Bauch, P. A. (2006). Reflective, ethical, and moral constructs in educational leadership preparation: effects on graduates' practices. *Journal of Educational Administration,* 44(5), 487. Retrieved from: http://proquest.umi.com/pqdweb?did=1105625181&Fmt=7&clientId=15403&RQT=309&VName=PQD

Stevenson, I. (2019). An improvement plan is not enough – you need a strategy. *Phi Delta Kappan, February 2019.* Retrieved from: https://kappan.org/school-improvement-plan-not-enough-you-need-strategy-stevenson/

Theoharis, G. (2007). Social justice educational leaders and resistance: Toward a theory of social justice leadership. *Educational Administration Quarterly,* 43(2), 221–258. https://doi.org/10.1177/0013161X06293717

Stage 2

Internship Plan Development

Following the review and analysis of the assessments in Stage 1, the intern will begin developing a draft of the initial internship plan. In this stage, the intern will choose activities under each of the NELP standard components (2.1), activities from the list of foundational skills (2.2), service to the district activities (2.3), and activities where the intern is a leadership role (2.4). Following the initial draft, the intern will meet with the district intern supervisor who may have additional or other activities to be included in the plan. Once the plan is approved by the school supervisor and program advisor, the intern may begin the activities.

It is normal for the intern plan to vary in time and effort between activities. For example, the intern may spend one hour in conducting and interview and 20 hours in leading a project or preparing and presenting a staff development workshop. The intent of this text is to provide the needed flexibility for the intern to address their individual needs, provide service to the school, and take advantage of unforeseen opportunities and circumstances. As such, numerous activities may be included in place of the activities in the text. Additionally, internship plans may be amended as unplanned opportunities and circumstances arise during the internship. Listed at the end of each leadership area is the following activity:

♦ Other related activities assigned or approved by your district supervisor and/or program advisor, or activities that are part of a larger project.

The final plan should have a significant percentage of experiences in leading versus observing, participating, or carrying out assigned tasks AND have a focus on increased student learning, overall district improvement, and developing self and others.

2.1 Activities to Meet National Standards

The following national standards describe what an entry-level district administrator should know and be able to do. The activities you select should be individualized based upon your strengths and weaknesses identified in your self-assessment. The district internship supervisor may adapt some activities or replace with other activities that meet this standard component. Some activities under a standard are "highly recommended" and should be included in the plan, if possible and applicable. Additional activities are listed for the intern to obtain a broader and more in-depth learning experience. Choose activities that will provide a significant degree of mastery of the standard components.

DOI: 10.4324/9781003299493-3

Standard 1

Vision, Mission, and Improvement

Candidates who successfully complete a district-level educational leadership preparation program understand and demonstrate the capacity to promote the current and future success and wellbeing of each student and adult by applying the knowledge, skills, and commitments necessary to collaboratively lead, design, and implement a district mission, vision, and process for continuous improvement that reflects a core set of values and priorities that include data use, technology, values, equity, diversity, digital citizenship, and community.

A district-level education leader must have the knowledge and skills to promote the success of every student through collaboratively leading, designing, and implementing a district mission, vision, and process for continuous improvement that reflects a core set of values and priorities. This includes knowledge of how to design, communicate, and evaluate a district mission and vision that reflects a core set of values and priorities and to lead district strategic planning and continuous improvement processes that engage diverse stakeholders in diagnosis, design, implementation, and evaluation.

NELP Standard Component 1.1

Understand and demonstrate the capacity to collaboratively design, communicate, and evaluate a district mission and vision that reflects a core set of values and priorities that include data use, technology, values, equity, diversity, digital citizenship, and community. The superintendent candidate should be able to:

♦ Evaluate existing mission and vision processes and statements.
♦ Collaboratively design an actionable district mission and vision attentive to such considerations as data use, technology, values, equity, diversity, digital citizenship, and community.
♦ Develop a comprehensive plan for communicating the mission and vision to multiple constituencies.

Discussion:

District leaders are responsible for the development and implementation of the district vision and mission statements. Since this responsibility entails creation of these assertions in some cases and the promotion and advancement of such declarations in all circumstances, the district leader must be proficient in the analysis, evaluation, updating, and communication of the district vision and mission statements. For these reasons, it is critically important that the district leader intern gain experience and skill in facilitating and guiding the development of the vision and mission statements. Likewise, the intern should seek to identify and acquire skills and strategies that will contribute to the exploitation of these guiding statements throughout the school organization. The vision and mission serve to "guide" school personnel in practice and future decision-making and communicate to all district stakeholders the focus

---

of district operations. In essence, the vision is the successful realization of the mission. The intern should observe and participate in the development or revision of the district vision and mission statements or lead the process of developing vision and mission statements for a sub-unit of the school district.

It is highly recommended that interns select activity a) as one of their chosen activities to demonstrate this skill component.

Choose activities below that you desire to include in the initial internship plan to meet the expectations of this national standard component. The district supervisor may adapt some activities or replace with other activities that meet this standard component. The majority of the activities are recommended for maximum learning and experience.

    a. Evaluate the current district vision and mission statements for evidence of reference to data use, technology, values, equity, diversity, digital citizenship, social justice, and community involvement. Describe the potential negative ramifications of omitting any of the above and make recommendations for how these might be included.

    b. Study the district's current process and calendar detailing when and how the vision and mission are reviewed, approved, and revised. Describe who is involved in the review and approval process, their level of involvement, and recommendations for improvement.

       1. Superintendent
       2. Board members
       3. Principals
       4. Teachers
       5. Staff
       6. Students
       7. Parents, community members, and/or other stakeholders

    c. Design a research-based process to effectively implement the district's vision and mission statements. Who would be involved and what strategies would you use?

    d. Evaluate the visibility of the district's vision and mission statements by reviewing district documents that are publicly accessible. Are the statements prominently displayed in district facilities and/or in district publications? Develop a comprehensive plan for communicating the mission and vision to multiple constituencies: Who, how, when, and where will you disseminate the plan? How will you ensure inclusion of all constituent groups?

    e. What behaviors have you observed from district administrators that promote the district's vision and mission? Identify barriers that hinder the district's vision and mission statements. Develop a set of recommendations that might be used to address identified barriers.

    f. Other related activities assigned or approved by your district supervisor and/or program advisor, or activities that are part of a larger project.

NELP Standard Component 1.2

Understand and demonstrate the capacity to lead district strategic planning and continuous improvement processes that engage diverse stakeholders in data collection, diagnosis, design, implementation, and evaluation. The superintendent candidate should be able to:

♦ Evaluate existing improvement processes.
♦ Develop a district-wide improvement process that includes data collection, diagnosis, design, implementation, and evaluation.
♦ Articulate a process for strategic planning.
♦ Develop an implementation plan to support the improvement process.

Discussion:

Given that district leaders are responsible for the development and implementation of a school district improvement plan, it is crucial that the intern gain the ability to understand, participate in, and lead the process of its development and use. Improvement plans are unique in that school district results may differ greatly when compared to state and district expectation. Additionally, school districts will vary when comparing geography, demographics, size, wealth, culture, community, and current student performance. In essence, the school district improvement plan is a roadmap to realize the district vision.

It is highly recommended that interns select activity a) as one of their chosen activities to demonstrate this skill component.

Choose activities below that you desire to include in the initial internship plan to meet the expectations of this national standard component. The district supervisor may adapt some activities or replace with other activities that meet this standard component. The majority of the activities are recommended for maximum learning and experience.

a. Review the current District Improvement Plan. Contact the person(s) responsible for the development of the plan, Describe the process used regarding a) timeline, b) persons involved, c) resources, d) data collected (i.e., student test scores, needs assessments, etc.), and e) strategies for approval, implementation, and evaluation. Note any concerns and/or recommendations.

b. Make a list of all district improvement activities undertaken during the past two years. Assess the progress made toward meeting the goals of the district improvement plan. List recommendations for greater progress considering leadership, communication, implementation, persons involved, and formative assessment.

c. Identify a high performing school district with similar demographics to your district and analyze the District Improvement Plans of the two districts. Identify similarities and differences of the two plans and note needed improvements to the plan of your district.

d. After reviewing your district's performance data, state academic performance report, human resources, budget, and all other district metrics, identify at least one area that you believe should be addressed in a long-term goal. Write a component of your district's strategic plan to address the area you have identified.

e. Analyze your school district's Strategic Plan and identify strengths and weaknesses of the plan. If your district does not have a strategic plan, you may utilize another district's plan. Research recommended elements of an effective Strategic Plan and review the content of your district's plan. Are all the elements in your district plan?

f. The intern should observe and/or participate in the development of the district improvement plan and the strategic plan, if possible.

g. Other related activities assigned or approved by your district supervisor and/or program advisor, or activities that are part of a larger project.

Standard 2

Ethics and Professional Norms

Candidates who successfully complete a district-level educational leadership preparation program understand and demonstrate the capacity to promote the current and future success and well-being of each student and adult by applying the knowledge, skills, and commitments necessary to understand and demonstrate the capacity to advocate for ethical decisions and cultivate professional norms and culture.

A district-level education leader must have the knowledge and skills to advocate for ethical decisions and cultivate professional norms and culture. This includes knowledge of how to reflect on, communicate about, and cultivate professional norms and culture and to evaluate and advocate for ethical and legal decisions. It also involves an understanding of how to model ethical behavior in their personal conduct and relationships and to cultivate ethical behavior in others.

NELP Standard Component 2.1

Understand and demonstrate the capacity to reflect on, communicate about, and cultivate professional dispositions and norms (i.e., equity, fairness, integrity, transparency, trust, collaboration, perseverance, reflection, lifelong learning, and digital citizenship) and professional district and school cultures. The superintendent candidate should be able to:

♦ Engage in reflective practice.
♦ Cultivate professional norms among diverse constituencies.
♦ Model and communicate professional norms (i.e., integrity, fairness, transparency, trust, equity, democracy, digital citizenship, diversity, inclusiveness, and the belief that each child can learn).
♦ Use professional norms as a basis for building organizational culture.

Discussion:

Successful school district leaders understand that actions speak louder than words and that district stakeholders are watching you and your actions, hoping that the leader demonstrates honesty, integrity, and fairness. The superintendent is expected to be a role model and should demonstrate professional behavior in both action and decisions. To be a "professional" in the eyes of others, the wise leader reflects on what others learn from their modeling of professional norms. Examples include whether the leader is seen to be honest, fair, and transparent, follows through with promises, keeps up with current issues and research in the field of educational leadership and learning, and makes decisions that represent the best interests of all students and district personnel. Attending school board meetings and watching the superintendent interact with school board members, staff, and constituents will reveal much about the individual and his or her leadership style.

It is highly recommended that interns select activity a) as one of their chosen activities to demonstrate this skill component.

Choose activities below that you desire to include in the initial internship plan to meet the expectations of this national standard component. The district supervisor may adapt some activities or replace with other activities that meet this standard component. The majority of the activities are recommended for maximum learning and experience.

  a. Meet with two or more respected district leaders to gather information on how they modeled and were able to:
     • Develop trust
     • Act with integrity
     • Model fairness
     • Lead with transparency
     • Use collaboration
     • Promote honesty
     • Support equity, diversity, and inclusiveness
     Reflect on your leadership behaviors. What specific behaviors do you plan to focus on and improve?
  b. Interview the district chief financial officer and ask for examples of district practices and policies which are intended to ensure transparency regarding the handling of taxpayer dollars. Identify corresponding district policies concerning business operations to determine the ethical process for purchasing products or services.
  c. Ask your Human Resources administrator to share examples of district policy and practice that are designed to foster diversity and equitable treatment among school district employees.
  d. Review the faculty handbook and board operating procedures. To what extent are professional norms addressed? Are all professional norms listed in the above activity a) addressed? What recommendations would you make for additions and/or improvement?
  e. Visit appropriate regional, state, and national organizations' websites that primarily represent superintendents. What are the current issues or topics addressed? What benefits are derived from membership and participation, i.e., conferences, newsletters/journals, training, networking, etc.? Is there a requirement for superintendent membership? What recommendations would you make for the level of involvement and participation by the superintendent in these different organizations?
  f. Other related activities assigned or approved by your district supervisor and/or program advisor, or activities that are part of a larger project.

NELP Standard Component 2.2

Understand and demonstrate the capacity to evaluate and advocate for ethical and legal decisions. The superintendent candidate should be able to:

♦ Evaluate ethical dimensions of complex issues, including stewardship and use of district resources.
♦ Analyze decisions in terms of established ethical frameworks.
♦ Advocate for ethical decisions.

Discussion:

School district leaders are faced with making decisions, almost nonstop, throughout the day. To ensure that their numerous decisions are ethical and legal, they must have a full understanding of ethical behavior, school board policy, and school law. They must develop a habit of "reflection in practice" while leading the decision-making process. When a decision is made and the superintendent has an opportunity to observe the result of his/her decision, time should be given to reflect on the result. The leader understands that ethical and legal decisions not only keep students, parents, faculty, and the school district out of legal trouble, but they also protect and ensure the rights of all stakeholders.

The intern is "forewarned" that ignorance of the law and failure to act ethically is not an acceptable excuse and may result in harm to self and others, and termination of an educational leadership career. It is strongly advised that much time and thought be given to the activities in this component. In today's complex society it is often a prudent decision on the part of the superintendent to delay making a quick decision, which is wanted by everyone seeking a decision, and wait until you research the issue and perhaps seek a legal opinion. It is better to be "right" than "quick".

It is highly recommended that interns select activity a) as one of their chosen activities to demonstrate this skill component.

Choose activities below that you desire to include in the initial internship plan to meet the expectations of this national standard component. The district supervisor may adapt some activities or replace with other activities that meet this standard component. The majority of the activities are recommended for maximum learning and experience.

a. Review your state's code of ethics for school board members. Did your district adopt the state code of ethics, develop their own, or neglect to follow one? What district policies are in place to address issues of integrity, fairness, and ethics for administrators and the board? What policies or laws govern the acceptance of gifts by the school superintendent and district board members?

b. Interview the district Chief Financial Officer to determine the total funds allocated in the current budget for representation by the district's attorney and for any other legal representation of the district such as special education lawyers, litigation attorneys, or human resource representation or other specialized representation of district interests. If possible, review the actual expenditures for all such representation for the past three years. Cite the budgetary formula for determining normal annual legal costs and unanticipated costs. Note recommendations for limiting legal expenses.

c. Interview an appropriate administrator from the taxing entity that includes your school district. Seek information about the history of taxation in your district, how taxes or millage is determined, and how tax rates are legally adopted.

d. Using the most current approved budget for your school district, analyze and compare expenditures for the following programs:

Athletics vs. Music/Fine Arts

Regular Education vs. Special Education

Career & Technology Programs vs. Extracurricular Activities

Are there legal or equity issues associated with these program expenditures (such as Title IX and others)? How do you plan to monitor legal and ethical budget decisions when you become a superintendent?

e. Review policies in your school district that address fair and equitable treatment of personnel. Describe the protocol for consideration of personnel grievances in your district.

f. Review the Open Meetings Act (OMA). What are the requirements for publicly posting an agenda for a board meeting? What must be shared in that posting? Gather from a district leader, common examples where board members might be in violation of the OMA.

g. Other related activities assigned or approved by your district supervisor and/or program advisor, or activities that are part of a larger project.

NELP Standard Component 2.3

Understand and demonstrate the capacity to model ethical behavior in their personal conduct and relationships and to cultivate ethical behavior in others. The superintendent candidate should be able to:

♦ Model ethical behavior in their personal conduct and relationships with others.
♦ Cultivate ethical behavior in others.

Discussion:

Most states and professional associations develop and publish a code (standards) of ethics and expect educators to adhere to these expectations. While a code of ethics is informative and essential, adhering to ethical expectations provides leadership and an example for others. It is crucial that the intern communicate and model high expectations for himself/herself and others that comprise the district administrative team. Ethical and moral behavior is extremely important as many people will judge how and why a decision is made as being more important than the actual decision. The superintendent intern is advised to consider their personal ethics in relationships in the school district and in their personal life as well. Moral and personal ethical practice is a habit of thought and behavior. Developing this habit is essential to successful leadership.

It is highly recommended that interns select activity a) as one of their chosen activities to demonstrate this skill component.

Choose activities below that you desire to include in the initial internship plan to meet the expectations of this national standard component. The district supervisor may adapt some activities or replace with other activities that meet this standard component. The majority of the activities are recommended for maximum learning and experience.

a. Identify policies that address the importance of ethical behavior among the district's leadership team (superintendent and board members). Refer to the Board of Trustees Operating Procedures and Code of Conduct and the state code of conduct for school administrators. Attend board meetings and document behavior for adherence to procedure and policy.

b. Interview several current or former district leaders. Ascertain what actions they took that resulted in influencing ethical behavior in others? Identify and describe at least five personal attributes that a superintendent should demonstrate to emphasize the importance of ethical behavior.

c. Reflect on your individual leadership style and attributes. In what ways do you demonstrate/model ethical and professional behavior? Cite additional or alternative practices you can make to cultivate ethical behavior in others.

d. Other related activities assigned or approved by your district supervisor and/or program advisor, or activities that are part of a larger project.

Standard 3

Equity, Inclusiveness, and Cultural Responsiveness

Candidates who successfully complete a district-level educational leadership preparation program understand and demonstrate the capacity to promote the current and future success and well-being of each student and adult by applying the knowledge, skills, and commitments necessary to develop and maintain a supportive, equitable, culturally responsive, and inclusive district culture.

A district-level education leader must have the knowledge and skills to develop and maintain a supportive, equitable, culturally responsive, and inclusive district culture. This includes knowledge of how to cultivate and advocate for a supportive and inclusive district culture and evaluate, cultivate, and advocate for each student in the district having equitable access to safe and nurturing schools and other resources and opportunities necessary for success. It also involves an understanding of how to evaluate, advocate, and cultivate equitable instructional and behavior support practices among teachers and staff.

NELP Standard Component 3.1

Understand and demonstrate the capacity to evaluate, cultivate, and advocate for a supportive and inclusive district culture. The superintendent candidate should be able to:

♦ Evaluate district culture.
♦ Use research and evidence to design and cultivate a supportive and inclusive district culture.
♦ Advocate for a supportive and inclusive district culture.

Discussion:

Successful school district leaders understand the importance and necessity of being fully aware of the history, traditions, values, and practices of the district and comprise current school culture. They accept the responsibility of assessing the culture and developing and implementing strategies to provide and support a positive, safe, supportive, and respectful learning environment for all students, staff, faculty, and all stakeholders. A superintendent that understands the importance of district culture, questions the policies and practices of the district to determine if they are aligned with supporting the desired culture. When policy or practice is inconsistent with a positive, safe, supportive, and respectful environment, then a change process should be initiated. Having the courage to initiate change, especially when others may not embrace it, is a requirement for enlightened leadership.

It is highly recommended that interns select activity a) as one of their chosen activities to demonstrate this skill component.

Choose activities below that you desire to include in the initial internship plan to meet the expectations of this national standard component. The district supervisor may adapt some activities or replace with other activities that meet this standard component. The majority of the activities are recommended for maximum learning and experience.

a. Convene a focus group of employees from multiple campuses across the district. Ask the focus group to respond to two questions:
   1. What does it take to create and maintain a positive culture of learning across the district?
   2. What actions can we take to foster an improved culture in our district?
   3. What should be changed or not done to foster a culture of learning and acceptance?

b. Conduct a review of district extracurricular activities participation (athletics, clubs, drama, music, special interest, etc.). Evaluate the findings to ascertain whether the demographic enrollment of the district is reflected in the participation of extracurricular activities.

c. Identify three initiatives, activities, performances, and/or communications that contribute to a positive district culture: respect for others, concern for the well-being of others, commitment to excellence in all district subpopulations, equitable distribution of resources, and other attributes and characteristics which you judge to be effective in the creation and maintenance of a positive district culture.

d. Identify a research-based process for fostering school district cultural change and promoting an inclusive district culture.

e. Analyze your school district's Student Code of Conduct. Does the Student Code of Conduct reflect a caring, responsive, and inclusive district culture? What recommendations would you propose?

f. Identify recent school district strategies which solicited parent and community participation in decision-making associated with a supportive district culture. To what degree have the strategies been successful? What are the major obstacles limiting greater success?

g. Review district curriculum to determine the status of equity and cultural responsiveness in your district. Conduct an audit identifying current strategies utilized by your school district to provide multilingual communication to all constituent groups.

h. Other related activities assigned or approved by your district supervisor and/or program advisor, or activities that are part of a larger project.

NELP Standard Component 3.2

Understand and demonstrate the capacity to evaluate, cultivate, and advocate for equitable access to safe and nurturing schools and the opportunities and resources, including instructional materials, technologies, classrooms, teachers, interventions, and adult relationships, necessary to support the success and well-being of each student. The superintendent candidate should be able to:

♦ Evaluate sources of inequality and bias in the allocation of educational opportunities and resources, including instructional materials, technologies, classrooms, teachers, interventions, and adult relationships.

♦ Cultivate the equitable use of educational resources and opportunities through procedures, guidelines, norms, and values.

♦ Advocate for equitable access to educational resources, procedures, and opportunities.

Discussion:

School systems in the US have a long history of inequities regarding educational resources and opportunities for all students. Despite numerous state and federal laws that address this situation, disparities remain due to differences in wealth, parental educational level, home environment, bias, culture, and school district practice. Without strong leadership and advocacy for equal educational resources and opportunities, students facing greater challenges will fall further and further behind their peers. The intern is advised to be fully aware of and take advantage of laws, policies, and opportunities for addressing inequity and devise strategies and advocate for the students in most need.

It is highly recommended that interns select activity a) as one of their chosen activities to demonstrate this skill component.

Choose activities below that you desire to include in the initial internship plan to meet the expectations of this national standard component. The district supervisor may adapt some activities or replace with other activities that meet this standard component. The majority of the activities are recommended for maximum learning and experience.

a. Review the district budget, personnel assignments, technology allocation, and other resources being provided to schools in the district and analyze the data for equity issues. Compare school budgets between two or more high schools, middle schools, and/or elementary schools. List all perceived inequities and discuss with your site supervisor the rationale for any discrepancies.

b. Interview the district Special Education Director to determine if your district can meet Individual Education Plan requirements for each special education student. In cases where students may have severe mental, emotional, or physical disabilities, describe the process and costs for contracting with outside organizations or agencies.

c. Interview the Title I Coordinator or another person responsible for the acquisition and distribution of Title Funds in your district. Describe the process used to obtain funding, eligibility of those receiving funding, and requirements of annual federal reporting. What is the perceived impact of the funding on student learning?

d. Conduct a safety review for one facility in your school district, utilizing the National Clearinghouse for Educational Facilities Checklist, or other recognized safety checklist document.

e. Review your district's facilities for compliance with federal regulations involving handicap accessibility. Does the district operate any facilities that are not in compliance due to "grandfathered" codes?

f. Review athletic facilities in the school district. Does the quality of facilities for boy sports and girl sports differ? If so, what is the justification for the disparity?

g. Other related activities assigned or approved by your district supervisor and/or program advisor, or activities that are part of a larger project.

NELP Standard Component 3.3

Understand and demonstrate the capacity to evaluate, advocate, and cultivate equitable, inclusive, and culturally responsive instructional and behavior support practices among teachers and staff. The superintendent candidate should be able to:

- ◆ Evaluate root causes of inequity and bias.
- ◆ Develop district policies or procedures that cultivate equitable, inclusive, and culturally responsive practice among teachers and staff.
- ◆ Advocate for culturally responsive instructional and behavior support practices among district staff and across district schools.
- ◆ Cultivate culturally responsive instructional and behavior support practices across the district and its schools.

Discussion:

Every educator, through life's teachings and experience, has developed biases and they become part of the belief system that guides their behavior and action. Implicit bias about some student characteristics can result in lowered academic and social expectations and the acceptance of failure for non-mastery due to issues of bias regarding gender, race, religion, age, or sexual orientation. As the school district superintendent, it is your responsibility to guide and provide professional development for teachers and staff that address personal bias and expectations for student performance. School districts with predominately one-size-fits-all curriculum and instructional strategies may unintentionally instill and promote further bias and negatively impact student success. Successful school district leaders must confront personal bias, model appropriate behavior, and train faculty and staff to address the importance of providing a culturally responsive instructional program for students. Do you have the courage to initiate this difficult conversation with others?

It is highly recommended that interns select activity a) as one of their chosen activities to demonstrate this skill component.

Choose activities below that you desire to include in the initial internship plan to meet the expectations of this national standard component. The district supervisor may adapt some activities or replace with other activities that meet this standard component. The majority of the activities are recommended for maximum learning and experience.

- a. Compile a list of activities or other practices in the district that teach awareness, respect, and appreciation for other cultures and ethnic groups. Identify district plans to make curricular/program changes to address diversity, equity, and inclusion in the school district.
- b. Review district data on disciplinary actions, i.e., office referrals, suspensions, and expulsions, and compare totals of differing demographics, i.e., gender, ethnicity, with percentages of similar students in the district.

   c. Identify potential causes of inequity and bias in your school district. Review current learning outcomes/curricular standards addressing diversity, equity, and inclusion. List recommendations to assist in reducing inequity and bias.

   d. Document examples of your district's professional development program that focus on teacher/administrator understanding of equitable, culturally responsive, and inclusive instructional practices.

   e. Identify school district practice and/or programs that promote the inclusion of parents and community members in understanding the importance of culturally responsive instructional and behavioral support practices.

   f. Other related activities assigned or approved by your district supervisor and/or program advisor, or activities that are part of a larger project.

Standard 4

Learning and Instruction

Candidates who successfully complete a district-level educational leadership preparation program understand and demonstrate the capacity to promote the current and future success and well-being of each student and adult by applying the knowledge, skills, and commitments necessary to evaluate, design, cultivate, and implement coherent systems of curriculum, instruction, data systems, supports, assessment, and instructional leadership.

A district-level leader must have the knowledge and skills to evaluate, design, cultivate, and implement coherent systems of curriculum, instruction, supports, assessment, and instructional leadership. This includes knowledge of how to evaluate, design, and implement curricula, instructional technologies, and other supports for student programs and how to evaluate, design, and cultivate systems of support, coaching, and professional development for principals and other school and district leaders. It also involves an understanding of how to design, implement, and evaluate coherent and technically, developmentally, and culturally appropriate systems of curriculum, resources, supports, instruction, assessments, and data collection, management, and analysis that support student learning and well-being, instruction, and instructional leadership.

NELP Standard Component 4.1

Understand and demonstrate the capacity to evaluate, design, and implement high-quality curricula, the use of technology, and other services and supports for academic and non-academic student programs. The superintendent candidate should be able to:

- ♦ Evaluate (a) curricula, use of technology, and other supports, (b) academic and non-academic systems, and (c) coordination among systems and supports.
- ♦ Use research and evidence to propose designs and implementation strategies for improving coordination and coherence among (a) curricula, instructional technologies, and other supports, and (b) academic and non-academic systems.

Discussion:

Principals, curriculum directors, and perhaps even department chairs and teachers, are often given responsibilities to design and develop district curriculum that aligns with district, state, and national standards and expectations for student success. However, in most cases, it is the superintendent of the district that most stakeholders hold accountable for district performance. The superintendent must be able to evaluate the curriculum and assess instructional strategies and appraise the efficiency and effectiveness of technology in the design and implementation of a district curriculum that contributes to a meaningful and expedient academic experience for each student. In addition, the superintendent is charged with the responsibility of determining the extent to which all district programs and district systems do or do not support and contribute to such an experience for each student.

In conjunction with other district staff, consultants, and experts, the superintendent is expected to utilize the findings of his own assessment as well as state and district data, research on best practices, and other relevant findings to propose strategies for improving the district's capacity to support and improve the district's curriculum and the execution of that body of knowledge and strategies for implementation. The superintendent's efforts in this area of responsibility must foster a team approach to the support of teaching and learning and to the identification of specific learning materials and development of teaching strategies and technologies that manifest best practices in helping all students to learn and retain information and skills that are critical to their long-term academic success.

In short, the superintendent is responsible for carefully evaluating the district's program of study and must work closely with others in the district and outside the district to ensure that students are taught the right material that aligns with state and national standards, that best practices in teaching are consistently implemented, that technology and other components of district services provide support for teachers, specifically and effectively contribute to the long range success of students and, ultimately, that the district is engaged in an incessant effort to improve this area of the district's endeavor.

It is highly recommended that interns select activity a) as one of their chosen activities to demonstrate this skill component.

Choose activities below that you desire to include in the initial internship plan to meet the expectations of this national standard component. The district supervisor may adapt some activities or replace with other activities that meet this standard component. The majority of the activities are recommended for maximum learning and experience.

a. Using all academic performance metrics for your school district, identify three areas of strength in district performance, and identify three areas in need of improvement from the perspective of the district performance. Be sure to justify/support your findings.

b. Interview an Assistant Superintendent for Curriculum and Instruction or some other district level administrator with similar responsibility. Ask the person whom you are interviewing to provide examples of horizontal and vertical curriculum alignment. Write a 2-page reflection of your understanding of *horizontal curriculum alignment* and *vertical curriculum alignment* based on your interview.

c. Evaluate your district's use of technology and describe efforts to support academic and non-academic programs. Refer to the International Society for Technology in Education (ISTE) standards as you evaluate your own district. Develop a written summary of your district's current use of technology and other ways that the district supports academic and non-academic programs. Include a final section which suggests ways that the district could utilize new technology or could use existing technology more efficiently and ways that the district could enhance support of academic and non-academic programs.

d. Participate as a member of the textbook adoption committee for the school district or if participation is not possible, interview the textbook committee chairman to determine the operations of the committee. Write a summary of your experience if you can serve on the textbook adoption committee or write a summary of the operations of the textbook committee based on your interview with the committee chairman if you are unable to serve on the committee personally.

e. Other related activities assigned or approved by your district supervisor and/or program advisor, or activities that are part of a larger project.

NELP Standard Component 4.2

Understand and demonstrate the capacity to collaboratively evaluate, design, and cultivate systems of support, coaching, and professional development for educators, educational professionals, and school and district leaders, including themselves, that promote reflection, digital literacy, distributed leadership, data literacy, equity, improvement, and student success. The superintendent candidate should be able to:

- ♦ Use research and data to evaluate the coordination, coherence, and relevance of the district's systems of support, coaching, and professional development for educators, educational professionals, and leaders.
- ♦ Use research to propose designs and implementation strategies for cultivating systems of support and professional development that promote reflection, digital literacy, distributed leadership, data literacy, equity, improvement, and student success.

Discussion:

New superintendents "inherit" current personnel employed by the school district as well as existing systems and structures designed to support and develop district employees and programs. To ensure growth and development among all faculty, administrators, and staff, the superintendent must take responsibility for the development and implementation of a coherent system of coaching, training, professional development, and reinforcement for all district employees and staff. Such a system is likely to cultivate additional systems of support among district employees and should generate meaningful, effective professional development which targets the skills of reflection, digital literacy, and leadership and promotes equity, improvement, and success among students of the district as well as contributing to the attainment of district goals and the vision and mission of the district. A coherent system of support must be aligned to district goals and objectives and must be relevant and meaningful to the employees who are benefactors of such support. The superintendent, in collaboration with other district staff, must analyze student performance data and other indicators of success to develop and lead a professional development agenda specifically designed to address academic and instructional deficits in need of improvement.

Effective superintendents and successful school districts make every effort to base professional development topics and activities on the analysis of success indicators rather than personal preferences or individual perceptions of need. A reliance on personal preference or individual perception often leads to professional development that is not truly aligned to the needs of the district and, specifically, are often not effective in the improvement of student performance. Effective superintendents are interested in knowing that the limited resources of the district that are allocated to professional development are effectively and efficiently providing district employees with the knowledge, tools, materials, and support that are needed to enhance the likelihood that students will learn and will experience success in the classrooms of the district.

It is highly recommended that interns select activity a) as one of their chosen activities to demonstrate this skill component.

Choose activities below that you desire to include in the initial internship plan to meet the expectations of this national standard component. The district supervisor may adapt some activities or replace with other activities that meet this standard component. The majority of the activities are recommended for maximum learning and experience.

a. Conduct a review of upcoming professional development activities to be implemented in the school district. How many of the activities are instruction related? Create a chart listing all the upcoming professional development activities in your district for the upcoming semester or for the summer. In the chart, list the name, date, and description of each professional development activity and include a column which identifies the activity as "instructional" or "non-instructional" based on the information provided in the notice or based on other knowledge you have of the content of the professional development activity. Examples of "non-instructional" activities may include activities such as "How to use the laminator machine" or "How to submit grades in the district computer program" or "How to conduct meaningful conferences with parents", and other activities not directly related to instruction. While any of these activities could contribute to improved instruction, many of them have no direct correlation to instruction. Finally, be sure to include a summary of your analysis that identifies the percentage of activities which you deem to be directly associated with instruction versus those activities that may not be directly associated with the instructional phase of education.

b. Analyze the professional development activities and offerings in the district during the past year. Identify the top three areas of professional development across the district based on number of hours of professional development offered. Write a one-page summary of your analysis and include a paragraph in which you draw inferences from your findings.

c. Interview the district level administrator that is primarily responsible for professional development planning in your school district and identify the process used to identify district priorities. Summarize your findings in a flow chart or other graphic which outlines the process.

d. Determine whether your district maintains a professional library (online or physical). If so, evaluate the library holdings and make recommendations for new acquisitions to enhance the capacity of the library and ensure access by all district professionals. If not, evaluate the professional library holdings of a nearby district and make recommendations for the development of a professional library in your district. Keep budget and time constraints in mind as you complete this activity. Document your evaluation, findings, and recommendations in a memo to the district director of professional development.

e. Other related activities assigned or approved by your district supervisor and/or program advisor, or activities that are part of a larger project.

NELP Standard Component 4.3

Understand and demonstrate the capacity to design, implement, and evaluate a developmentally appropriate, accessible, and culturally responsive system of assessments and data collection, management, and analysis that support instructional improvement, equity, student learning and well-being, and instructional leadership. The superintendent candidate should be able to:

♦ Evaluate the quality of formative and summative assessments of student learning.
♦ Evaluate coordination and coherence among academic and non-academic assessments and use data from these sources to support instructional improvement, student learning and well-being, and instructional leadership.
♦ Use research to propose designs and implementation strategies for district-wide assessment systems that are culturally responsive and accessible.

Discussion:

The superintendent must oversee the development and implementation of formative and summative assessments of student learning and ensure the coordination and use of data from those assessments in making decisions related to the support of instructional improvement, student learning, instructional leadership, and allocation of district resources for these purposes. The superintendent must rely on expertise within and without the district as well as relevant academic research to design and implement strategies that create assessment systems that consider cultural responsiveness and accessibility for all students.

Given the critical nature of decisions being driven by district assessments, it is incumbent upon the superintendent to expect staff to regularly screen assessments for cultural bias and accessibility issues through a careful analysis of performance data and standard test analysis tools such as item analysis and item validation protocols. In addition, it is important that the superintendent is confident that district leaders have been appropriately trained and prepared to monitor the administration of district assessments, that they have the necessary prerequisites to interpret assessment results, and that district leaders have the capacity to utilize student performance data, both local and state, to guide decision-making in the instructional arena and to advocate for student success.

It is highly recommended that interns select activity a) as one of their chosen activities to demonstrate this skill component.

Choose activities below that you desire to include in the initial internship plan to meet the expectations of this national standard component. The district supervisor may adapt some activities or replace with other activities that meet this standard component. The majority of the activities are recommended for maximum learning and experience.

a. Interview the district administrator responsible for district curriculum and instruction. Ask the administrator to provide an example of the most recent district instructional strategy implemented as a result of analysis of student performance data. Write a summary of your interview in which you outline the specific instructional strategy that was implemented, summarize the timeline for implementation, the plan for evaluation of the new strategy, and the success indicators which will be used. Include a discussion of any formative assessments that may be planned for the purpose of considering adjustments or changes to the instructional strategy.

b. Identify state and federal reporting requirements of your school district by reviewing appropriate school district documents or interviewing appropriate personnel, i.e., special education director, federal programs director or designee, etc. Develop a list of all reports, what data is being requested on each report, who is responsible for each report, and when each report is submitted.

c. Analyze the qualifying criteria for advanced academic courses in your district. Do the criteria enable equitable student opportunities? Write a one-page summary of your analysis and your interpretation of those findings. Be sure to address the issue of equitable opportunities for all students.

d. Read the PDK "Classroom Tips" newsletter written by Laura Greenstein, the founder of the "Assessment Network". Reflect on ways to improve and enhance assessment that is culturally sensitive in your district. Greenstein, L. (2011, December). Creating assessments for all learners. *"Classroom Tips" A PDK Newsletter*. The article can be accessed at the following link:
http://www.pdkmembers.org/members_online/publications/ClassTips/Tips_
Dec11.pdf.

e. Utilizing the published state accountability data, identify 1) graduation rate, 2) student performance scores, or 3) college readiness comparison based on SAT/ ACT scores for the most recent two years. Write a summary of your findings and share your interpretation of the findings in terms of district performance compared to state performance and any trends that may be inferred from the data.

f. If you utilize benchmark testing in your school district, identify the benefits associated with utilizing this data as an assessment tool in reviewing district curriculum and student learning. Write a 2-page summary of the benefits and your perception of the benefits of utilization of this data as an assessment tool.

g. Select a high school in your school district and conduct a participation audit of advanced, dual-credit, and AP courses based on student gender, race, and at-risk designation. Create a chart which outlines your findings and write a one-page summary of your findings. Be sure to include a paragraph with your own inferences from the findings.

h. Other related activities assigned or approved by your district supervisor and/or program advisor, or activities that are part of a larger project.

NELP Standard Component 4.4

Understand and demonstrate the capacity to design, implement, and evaluate district-wide use of coherent systems of curriculum, instruction, assessment, student services, technology, and instructional resources that support the needs of each student in the district. The superintendent candidate should be able to:

♦ Engage appropriate staff in gathering, synthesizing, and using data to evaluate the quality, coordination, and coherence in and among the district's academic and non-academic services.

♦ Use research to propose designs and implementation strategies for improving coordination and coherence among the district's academic and non-academic systems.

♦ Use technology and performance management systems to monitor, analyze, and evaluate district curriculum, instruction, services, assessment practices, and results.

Discussion:

The final component in this standard appears to create an umbrella over a district-wide system designed to monitor the on-going evaluation of curriculum and the active engagement of district personnel and systems in the systematic collection, interpretation, and utilization of data. The superintendent must oversee and regularly monitor a system that accomplishes these tasks. The data collected from such an endeavor must be the basis for instructional decisions, budget decisions, personnel decisions, and district improvement initiatives. While state accountability and assessment systems provide an abundance of data that can and should be used to drive these decisions, it is also critically important that district personnel and systems be attuned to the unique characteristics and issues that are often specific to their district. For that reason, the superintendent must expect district leaders to regularly seek information and create systems to evaluate the performance of all students, all demographic groups, and all academic subpopulations in the district. In some cases, this may require special protocols or proprietary technology solutions to meet the challenge of monitoring student performance for every student and every subgroup engaged in every academic program of the district. Such information can then be used to drive district decision-making so that all students and all groups are likely to benefit.

It is highly recommended that interns select activity a) as one of their chosen activities to demonstrate this skill component.

Choose activities below that you desire to include in the initial internship plan to meet the expectations of this national standard component. The district supervisor may adapt some activities or replace with other activities that meet this standard component. The majority of the activities are recommended for maximum learning and experience.

a. Review and evaluate the use of data in your school district that drives curriculum decisions, planning, and professional development. Choose a recent curriculum decision, planning initiative, or professional development activity and summarize the data used to drive the endeavor. In the planning of the decision, initiative, or activity, include the role of the superintendent and the role of the board. Assess the effectiveness of the decision, initiative, or activity and provide any recommendations for improvement.

b. Form a focus group made up of instructional leaders, instructors, technology leaders, assessment, and instructional services personnel. Lead the focus group in a discussion of the district's coordination and coherence of instructional services, instruction, instructional monitoring, and assessment. Write a summary of your experience and include strengths and weaknesses identified by the group and recommendations for improvement that may have been discussed.

c. Review performance data to identify the most effective academic support program in your school district. Why is it the most effective? Write a summary of your findings and explain why you chose the program you did and what data supports your finding.

d. Conduct a comparison analysis of the three lowest areas of student performance in your school district to the planned professional development for the coming school year. Is the district focusing on the greatest instructional needs? Share your findings with the person responsible of professional development. The report may include graphics, charts, or other visuals.

e. Other related activities assigned or approved by your district supervisor and/or program advisor, or activities that are part of a larger project.

Standard 5

Community and External Leadership

Candidates who successfully complete a district-level educational leadership preparation program understand and demonstrate the capacity to promote the current and future success and well-being of each student and adult by applying the knowledge, skills, and commitments necessary to understand and engage families, communities, and other constituents in the work of schools and the district and to advocate for district, student, and community needs.

A district-level education leader must have the knowledge and skills to engage families, communities, and other constituents in the work of schools and the district and to advocate for district, student, and community needs. This includes knowledge of how to represent and support schools in engaging families in strengthening student learning in and out of school and to effectively collaborate, communicate, and engage community members, partners, and other constituencies in district matters that benefit learners, schools, and the district. It also involves an understanding of how to collaborate and communicate with members of the business, civic, and policy community so they can cultivate relationships and advocate for their district, student, and community needs.

NELP Standard Component 5.1

Understand and demonstrate the capacity to represent and support district schools in engaging diverse families in strengthening student learning in and out of school. The superintendent candidate should be able to:

♦ Represent the district and its schools.
♦ Support the efforts of district schools in engaging diverse families in strengthening student learning in and out of school.
♦ Make decisions about when and how to engage families.

Discussion:

As the superintendent of a school district, one accepts a responsibility to represent the school district in a manner that invites and encourages the involvement and support of community partners and creates a welcoming environment for all students and families of the district. The engagement of diverse families in the school program as well as a strong collaboration between parents and the school are significant factors in student success. Since learning occurs both in the school and outside the school, it is important for the school leader to foster a sense of community teamwork in engaging diverse parents and families in the education enterprise. A successful superintendent seeks out opportunities to recruit community partners in the active engagement of diverse families and other stakeholders and in supporting school initiatives and activities and in creating and maintaining environments conducive to student learning throughout the community. As the single most recognizable face of the school district in most communities, it is important that the superintendent commit appropriate time, energy, and effort to this endeavor.

It is highly recommended that interns select activity a) as one of their chosen activities to demonstrate this skill component.

Choose activities below that you desire to include in the initial internship plan to meet the expectations of this national standard component. The district supervisor may adapt some activities or replace with other activities that meet this standard component. The majority of the activities are recommended for maximum learning and experience.

a. Prepare a presentation for a group of teachers or governing board of the district to communicate a summary of the complex issues associated with poverty and other disadvantages and the effects of these circumstances on families, community, children, and learning. Use specific examples from the local context, as well as state and national data for comparison and share recommendations for engaging families from all subpopulations in the education and growth of students. Be sure to cite references and be sure that citations comply with research standards.

b. Make a list of strategies used in the district to solicit engagement of diverse families and community members and business and industry partners in the support of student achievement. Use the list to create a WORD CLOUD to help recall the many ways that schools in your district attempt to foster engagement of families, business, and community.

c. Collaborate with the Public Relations Officer in your school district to craft a "Talking Points" outline which can be used by any district employee to make a presentation to any service organization or community club. The presentation talking points should focus on district achievements and the celebration of student successes and on the needs of the district which may require additional tax dollars, reinforced support from the state or national government, and ways that community members can support the school mission.

d. Develop a survey instrument that solicits parents' and other district stakeholder opinions of the school district and its efforts to communicate with all constituents. Randomly select individuals representing as many diverse constituencies as possible and conduct telephone/email interviews/correspondence. Analyze the perceptions of each group.

e. Select a family in your district which represents diverse circumstances and conduct a case study to determine best practices for supporting and involving the family in school programs and in student learning. For this activity, seek a family that represents the following:
   • Willing to participate in your case study.
   • Multiple children in the school district – varying age groups.
   • Low SES – free lunch or other indicators as identified by the site supervisor.
   • Other subpopulations as approved by the site supervisor.

f. Other related activities assigned or approved by your district supervisor and/or program advisor, or activities that are part of a larger project.

NELP Standard Component 5.2

Understand and demonstrate the capacity to understand, engage, and effectively collaborate and communicate with, through oral, written, and digital means, diverse families, community members, partners, and other constituencies to benefit learners, schools, and the district. The superintendent candidate should be able to:

♦ Develop systems and processes designed to support district personnel's understanding of diverse families, community members, partners, and other constituencies.

♦ Collaborate with diverse community members, partners, and other constituencies.

♦ Foster regular, two-way communication with community members, partners, and other constituencies.

♦ Develop communication for oral, written, and digital distribution targeted to a diverse stakeholder community.

♦ Engage community members, partners, and other constituents in district efforts.

Discussion:

Superintendents must be aware of community resources available to help students and faculty members and to engage families in the education process. Partnership opportunities will vary with each school within the district and developing strategies to effectively communicate the importance of active engagement and partnership opportunities will be important. In large school districts, the strategies may vary as constituent groups often have unique preferences. What works for constituents in one school attendance zone may not be effective in another. This standard component emphasizes the importance of communicating the needs of the district to others as well as the importance of developing positive relationships with agencies and organizations and being knowledgeable of their resources and services. School districts that attempt to "go it alone" when facing complex issues will not be as successful as districts that seek support from those with available resources.

Superintendents must ensure adequate training and growth opportunities for district staff to understand and appreciate the unique challenges of diverse families and must set expectations for regular two-way communication between staff and community stakeholders. The superintendent must support efforts to communicate key district initiatives, activities, and announcements in various formats and languages that can be accessed and understood by a high percentage of the school community.

It is highly recommended that interns select activity a) as one of their chosen activities to demonstrate this skill component.

Choose activities below that you desire to include in the initial internship plan to meet the expectations of this national standard component. The district supervisor may adapt some activities or replace with other activities that meet this standard component. The majority of the activities are recommended for maximum learning and experience.

a. Identify and describe at least three strategies/activities from your district that are designed to encourage parent and community member participation/involvement in the mission of the school district. Include a short summary of each strategy and use pictures, hand-outs, announcements, or other district artifacts to verify your identification of three strategies.

b. Work with the district public relations officer to develop and implement regularly distributed newsletter to district constituents (parents, taxpayers, business owners, etc.). Focus the newsletter on school activities, celebration of student successes, and attempts to engage the diverse family population of the district in school activities and in the support of learning for all students. Include a copy or copies of the newsletter in the internship log. Be sure to summarize the various formats in which the newsletter is published, i.e., electronic, paper, oral, and other language versions, etc.).

c. Collaborate with district personnel to design a billboard that will draw attention to the district mission and seek support from school families, business owners, and other community constituents.

d. Describe your district's organized approach to scheduling teacher/parent conferences. If your district does not have a comprehensive program, develop a proposal that could be presented to the superintendent or designated administrator(s) advocating for program implementation.

e. Participate in an event in your school district that honors volunteers throughout the district. If your district does not sponsor an event, develop a presentation advocating the creation of an appropriate event. Describe the event in detail if you participated in the event or include a copy of your presentation proposal if your district does not currently sponsor such an event.

f. Participate in your district's facilitation of a "career day" event for the purpose of providing student interaction with representatives of higher education, military, job, and apprentice opportunities, etc. If your district does not provide a "career day" event, develop a presentation that would advocate for the implementation of an event. Describe the event in detail if you participated in the event and include hand-outs, posters, and announcements as artifacts from the district.

g. Other related activities assigned or approved by your district supervisor and/or program advisor, or activities that are part of a larger project.

NELP Standard Component 5.3

Understand and demonstrate the capacity to communicate through oral, written, and digital means within the larger organizational, community, and political contexts and cultivate relationships with members of the business, civic, and policy community in support of their advocacy for district, school, student, and community needs. The superintendent candidate should be able to:

♦ Conduct a needs assessment of the district, school, students, and community.
♦ Develop a plan for accessing resources that addresses district needs.
♦ Cultivate collaborative relationships with district constituencies.
♦ Develop oral, written, and digital communications targeted on the larger organizational, community, and political contexts.
♦ Advocate for district and community needs.

Discussion:

School districts cannot effectively function in isolation. A school district is one component of a larger, complex community of politics, finance, governance, and culture. An effective superintendent is well-versed in communication with other constituents of the community and is proficient in developing relationships with other community leaders. The ability to communicate effectively with other stakeholders in the community and an investment in strong relations with community leaders tend to serve the district well in times of crisis or need. A plea for information, or resources, or even influence, is more likely to be met with a welcome attitude when the superintendent has demonstrated effective communication skills with all community stakeholders and when the superintendent has devoted time and energy toward the building and maintaining of collegial and mutually respectful relationships with other leaders.

A wealth of information, support, and resources exist in the community to help meet the needs of the school district. Successful leaders understand the importance of forming relationships and communicating with other entities within the larger community, such as those at the regional, state, and federal level. As superintendent of a school district, one should be well-acquainted with the local newspaper's reporter or reporters assigned to education and should know how to contact local government leaders. In addition, the superintendent should have a relationship with the education liaison for the district's state representative, state senator, and congressional delegations. An even more preferential circumstance would see the superintendent in a personal relationship with each of these elected officials. A superintendent who can pick up the phone and speak personally with the state senator in Washington D.C. is much more likely to be successful in advocating for the district and for education in general than one who is unknown to the senator or to the senator's staff. Superintendents must be the primary advocate for the school district and for education in general and cultivating relationships is an important factor in accomplishing this component of superintendent responsibility.

It is highly recommended that interns select activity a) as one of their chosen activities to demonstrate this skill component.

Choose activities below that you desire to include in the initial internship plan to meet the expectations of this national standard component. The district supervisor may adapt some activities or replace with other activities that meet this standard component. The majority of the activities are recommended for maximum learning and experience.

a. Identify two to three major issues which you believe will be important to the ongoing success of your school district in the future. (For example, you may choose issues such as adequate funding for district programs, increased compensation for school employees, adequate insurance benefits for school employees, support for special populations, flexibility in the school day or school calendar, and a whole host of other issues of which you may be aware or may become aware.) Write a letter to your elected representative (state or federal) in which you advocate for the position which benefits the students and employees of your district. If you identify yourself as a representative of your school district, be sure to discuss the issue with your site-supervisor before sending the letter to ensure that your advocacy does not conflict with the efforts of your superintendent.

b. Invite your district public relations officer or other district leaders to join you in brainstorming ideas for recruiting local business engagement and support for school district initiatives. Document the list of ideas which is brainstormed and save the list for future consideration.

c. Identify teacher unions or associations that are active in your school district and describe their involvement with decision-making at the superintendent and board levels. Are the unions/associations consulted on a regular basis? What are the prominent issues of concern between the union/association and the superintendent and board? What strategies by the superintendent and board are most effective and developing a positive working relationship? If possible and approved by the district supervisor, meet with the union/association leader to ascertain their needs and desires of the district.

d. Identify the publications, media presentations, websites, etc., in your school district that are used to communicate with district constituencies. Identify the primary purpose and the intended audience of each. Create a chart or report which summarizes your findings.

e. Interview the person responsible for oversight of your district's Volunteer Program. After completing the interview, analyze your district's Volunteer Program and develop recommendations for improvement. If your district does not have an organized Volunteer Program, review programs in other districts and develop a presentation advocating for the creation of a program in your school district.

f. Organize a "Services for Students and Families Night" in your district. Invite presenters from local social, civic, and governmental entities that provide services to families so that parents may hear about programs that may be unknown to them. Include a copy of the announcement of the event, copies of correspondence with local social, civic, and governmental entities invited to participate, a summary of the event, and estimated participation in the event.

g. Other related activities assigned or approved by your district supervisor and/or program advisor, or activities that are part of a larger project.

Standard 6

Operations and Management

Candidates who successfully complete a district-level educational leadership preparation program understand and demonstrate the capacity to promote the current and future success and well- being of each student and adult by applying the knowledge, skills, and commitments necessary to develop, monitor, evaluate, and manage data-informed and equitable district systems for operations, resources, technology, and human capital management.

A district-level education leader must have the knowledge and skills to develop, monitor, evaluate, and manage district systems for operations, resources, and human capital management. This includes knowledge of how to design, communicate, implement, coordinate, and evaluate management, communication, technology, district-level governance, and operation systems that support schools in realizing the district's mission and vision and to design, communicate, advocate, implement, coordinate, and evaluate a district resourcing plan and support schools in developing their school-level resourcing plans. It also involves an understanding of how to develop, implement, and evaluate coordinated systems for hiring, retaining, supervising, developing, and cultivating school and district staff to support the district's collective instructional and leadership capacity.

NELP Standard Component 6.1

Understand and demonstrate the capacity to develop, communicate, implement, and evaluate data-informed and equitable management, communication, technology, governance, and operation systems at the district level to support schools in realizing the district's mission and vision. The superintendent candidate should be able to:

- ◆ Evaluate management and operation systems.
- ◆ Use data and research to propose designs for improving the coordination and impact of district management, communication, technology, governance, and operation systems.
- ◆ Communicate with relevant stakeholders about the relationship between the district's management, operation, and governance systems and the district's mission and vision.
- ◆ Develop an implementation plan to support improved district systems.

Discussion:

Effective superintendents understand the importance of programs that support academic and non-academic activities in the district. Have you considered the fact that your school district may be one of the largest employers in the community? It typically provides the largest food service operation, transportation system, maintenance program, custodial service, etc. Generally, the size and scope of these functions exceed other entities, both public and private, in the community. It is therefore important that the superintendent utilize data to determine efficiency and to develop strategies for continuous improvement for the purpose of accomplishing the district's mission and vision. Many do not realize that private businesses often outsource many of the functions that school districts provide internally (think human resources, business accounting, custodial services, maintenance, etc.). All these functions contribute to an effective school district. As the superintendent, you are charged with oversight of all district operations.

It is highly recommended that interns select activity a) as one of their chosen activities to demonstrate this skill component.

Choose activities below that you desire to include in the initial internship plan to meet the expectations of this national standard component. The district supervisor may adapt some activities or replace with other activities that meet this standard component. The majority of the activities are recommended for maximum learning and experience.

a. Review the district's safety plans and procedures. Include in that review an inspection of building evacuation drills in your school district. Compare your findings to safety requirements found in district policy and/or state requirements.

b. Interview the district maintenance director regarding the district's "preventive maintenance program". After the interview, describe how the program is implemented and create a summary of the maintenance director's strategy for prioritizing district resources to address health and safety issues such as fences, fire alarms, security cameras, door openers and closers, bathroom facilities, covered walkways, and many other examples. Based on the interview, what did you learn? What questions do you have regarding the maintenance at your district?

c. Interview the administrator responsible for custodians to find out what formal and informal training has been provided for custodians who are responsible for conducting the deep cleaning and sanitizing of all surfaces and facilities before students and staff enter the facility. In addition, investigate the personal safety protocol that has been communicated to custodians.

d. Review Board Policy that identifies how district goals are developed, adopted, and evaluated and interview the superintendent, asking for his/her comments as to how progress on goals is measured and for the timeline by which the board will determine if each goal has been met. Additionally discuss how these goals are disseminated to the faculty and staff. After the interview:

   • Describe the use of technology in your school district to support or disseminate data driven administrative or management decisions. Develop at least one suggestion that will improve the use of technology to support or disseminate management decisions.

   • Analyze three school district faculty handbooks and identify similarities and differences. Is there any additional information that you would include in the faculty handbooks?

e. Other related activities assigned or approved by your district supervisor and/or program advisor, or activities that are part of a larger project.

NELP Standard Component 6.2

Understand and demonstrate the capacity to develop, communicate, implement, and evaluate a data-based district resourcing plan and support schools in developing their school-level resourcing plans. The superintendent candidate should be able to:

- Use data to evaluate district resource needs and practices.
- Use research and data to design an equitable district resourcing plan and support schools in designing school resourcing plans that coordinate resources with needs.
- Communicate about district resources needs and plans.
- Develop an implementation plan for the district's resourcing plan.

Discussion:

The Board of Education approves the annual budget each year and works closely with the district superintendent during its development. Early in the budget development process, the superintendent works closely with the administrative team to ensure adequate resources are made available. Priorities are reflected in the budget that is developed and adopted. This includes the commitment of funds for personnel units. In summary, if you identify weak performance in academic or non-academic programs, review the budget. Include in the review the number of personnel assigned to each program. These data will reveal why a program is successful or struggling.

It is highly recommended that interns select activity a) as one of their chosen activities to demonstrate this skill component.

Choose activities below that you desire to include in the initial internship plan to meet the expectations of this national standard component. The district supervisor may adapt some activities or replace with other activities that meet this standard component. The majority of the activities are recommended for maximum learning and experience.

a. Interview the CFO of your school district and ask for a description of the process used to develop the district budget and how it is presented to the board of trustees for approval. After the interview, analyze your most recent district budget to determine the percentage of general revenue funds that is allocated to maintenance and operations budget. Conduct a similar analysis on two other budgets from districts comparable to yours (enrollment, geographic location, and/or tax base). Based on these analyses:
   - How does your district compare to other districts in the percentage of funds allocated for maintenance and operations?
   - Identify any areas of concern or adjustments you would propose.
b. Review the contents of board policy regarding meeting and publishing requirements of the district's proposed budget. Compare policy to the processes utilized in your school district.

   c. Describe a districtwide project that used an effective needs assessments, research-based data, and group process skills to build consensus regarding the alignment of resources with the district's vision. Provide examples of how the superintendent:
- Demonstrated the ability to manage time and to deploy financial and human resources effectively.
- Strategically communicated the district's resources and needs to constituency groups. (What district or community leaders would you include in the communication process?)

   d. Discuss with the superintendent the steps necessary to implement a voter-approved bond election to build a new school. What did you learn from the discussion? What additional information would you need to lead or assist with a bond election?

   e. Other related activities assigned or approved by your district supervisor and/or program advisor, or activities that are part of a larger project.

NELP Standard Component 6.3

Understand and demonstrate the capacity to develop, implement, and evaluate coordinated, data-informed systems for hiring, retaining, supervising, and developing school and district staff to support the district's collective instructional and leadership capacity. The superintendent candidate should be able to:

- Use data to evaluate district human resources needs.
- Use research and data to develop a district-level system for the hiring, retention, development, and supervision of school/district personnel.
- Evaluate candidates' materials for instructional and leadership positions.
- Implement systems of leadership supervision, evaluation, feedback, and support.

Discussion:

The quality of district personnel may be the most influential element in determining whether a school district achieves its mission and vision. The successful. superintendent commits quality time and resources to attract applicants, develops initiatives to retain effective employees, provides supervision that makes a difference, and is committed to enhancing instructional and leadership capacity. Because typical personnel costs comprise approximately 85% of the district's budget, a focus on quality professional development proves beneficial. What specific ideas do you have regarding the retention of a quality staff?

It is highly recommended that interns select activity a) as one of their chosen activities to demonstrate this skill component.

Choose activities below that you desire to include in the initial internship plan to meet the expectations of this national standard component. The district supervisor may adapt some activities or replace with other activities that meet this standard component. The majority of the activities are recommended for maximum learning and experience.

a. Interview the district administrator that oversees the human relations department in your school district. Seek information about recruitment, selection, and retention strategies to attract and keep quality personnel. Describe obstacles or challenges the district faces in competing with other school districts, i.e., compensation, location, demographics, etc. Develop a proposal for increasing the district's competitiveness. If possible, participate in a recruitment activity or meet with a member of a recruitment team and describe the process used and issues and concerns encountered.

b. Find out what metrics are reviewed regularly by your district's human resources department. Make a list of these metrics and write a short explanation of how each metric contributes to the efficiency and efficacy of the district.

1. Review the application process at your district.
2. Analyze the documents required for each applicant, the application itself, and any other pre-application screening such as a requirement for a one-page handwritten philosophy of education or other written commentary as to why one wants to work for this district.

3. Review applications for at least one school or leadership position which is currently advertised, ranking the candidates by existing standards.

4. Develop suggestions and/or recommendations for changes, adjustments, or deletions of items in the current process.

c. Review the current policy and practice for evaluating candidates for professional positions within the district. Describe the practice of involving other district employees in the evaluation and recommendation protocol and evaluate whether you believe the evaluation of potential new employees by other district employees is an efficient and effective protocol or make a recommendation you believe would be more effective.

d. Review the contracts of three different superintendents. Many superintendent contracts can be accessed at the district website. Do NOT to identify either the superintendent or the district. Label the contracts as A, B, & C. Evaluate each contract for the following:

1. Does the contract provide for membership fees for the superintendent in professional organizations? If so, are specific professional organizations identified and are there specific limitations on the district's financial support?

2. Does the contract specifically provide for support of the superintendent's travel? Is there a provision to pay for mileage, lodging, meals, airfare, and/or car rental or use of district vehicle?

3. Is there language in the contract that speaks specifically to the amount of time spent by the superintendent out of the district in attendance at professional meetings and/or serving in leadership positions in professional organizations?

4. Based on your analysis of each superintendent contract (A, B, or C), select the contract which you believe best supports the superintendent's professional growth and networking with other stakeholders. Explain the reasoning for your selection.

e. Review the state and local requirements for principal and central office personnel annual evaluations and obtain the instruments used for these positions in your school district. Compare the instruments to state and local requirements identifying any omissions or information inconsistent with requirements. Interview two or more persons evaluated by the superintendent or deputy, associate, or assistant superintendent and solicit their assessment of the forms and process used regarding objectivity/subjectivity, bias, accuracy, and degree of constructive advice for professional development. What recommendations for improvement would you make?

f. Become familiar with district policies that describe the different types of personnel contracts and other descriptions of employment associated with your school district. How does district policy describe: at-will employees, term contracts, probationary contracts, continuing contracts (tenure), and other forms of employment?

g. Other related activities assigned or approved by your district supervisor and/or program advisor, or activities that are part of a larger project.

Standard 7

Policy, Governance, and Advocacy

Candidates who successfully complete a district-level educational leadership preparation program, understand and demonstrate the capacity to promote the present and future success and well- being of students and district personnel by applying the knowledge, skills, and commitments necessary to cultivate relationships, lead collaborative decision making and governance, and represent and advocate for district needs in broader policy conversations.

A district-level education leader must have the knowledge and skills to cultivate relationships, lead collaborative decision making and governance, and represent and advocate for district needs in broader policy conversations. This includes an understanding of how to represent, communicate, collaborate, advocate, and cultivate a respectful and responsive relationship with a district's board of education focused on achieving the shared mission and vision of the district and to collaborate, design, communicate, implement, coordinate, cultivate, and evaluate effective systems for district governance that engage multiple stakeholder groups, including school and district personnel, families, community stakeholders, and board members. It also involves an understanding of how to evaluate and engage in decision making around, implement, and appropriately communicate about policy, laws, and regulations and how to evaluate, represent, and advocate for district needs and priorities within larger policy conversations.

NELP Standard Component 7.1

Understand and demonstrate the capacity to represent the district, advocate for district needs, and cultivate a respectful and responsive relationship with the district's board of education focused on achieving the shared mission and vision of the district. The superintendent candidate should be able to:

- ♦ Represent the district and its mission, strengths, and needs to the board of education.
- ♦ Cultivate a positive, respectful, and responsive relationship with the board.
- ♦ Advocate for board actions that will support the mission and vision of the district and meet district needs.

Discussion:

Developing a good, working relationship with the board of education is an important element of effective district leadership. The roles of the board and superintendent are different and are usually defined by law and policy. Shared respect and professional behavior are a must if the leadership team (board and superintendent) are to work together in accomplishing the mission and vision of the district. Developing a written document, often called Board/Superintendent Guidelines, is a great strategy to ensure mutual respect for the authority that is distinct to both parties. The document can also be used when a new superintendent is hired, or a new board member is elected during an orientation period. Most superintendents agree that providing opportunities for board members to know each other in settings other than board meetings is an excellent strategy. It usually results in opportunities to build relationships and establish team norms. How will you encourage mutual respect among the leadership team when you are hired as the superintendent?

It is highly recommended that interns select activity a) as one of their chosen activities to demonstrate this skill component.

Choose activities below that you desire to include in the initial internship plan to meet the expectations of this national standard component. The district supervisor may adapt some activities or replace with other activities that meet this standard component. The majority of the activities are recommended for maximum learning and experience.

a. Obtain a copy of the school district's document "*Superintendent and Board Operational Guidelines*" or similar document (the name of the document will vary from district to district). Conduct an analysis of the following items:
   - Development of the board meeting agenda.
   - Guidelines for board meeting decorum.
   - Electronic communications among board members.
   - Expectations for board members during bond and trustee elections.
   - Board member guidelines for interacting with school personnel.
   - Ethical guidelines for board members.
   - Board member travel guidelines and reimbursement policies.
   - Nepotism laws and guidelines for board members, and
   - Conflict of interest oaths and forms.

   If your school district does not have a document providing information on the items listed above, interview an appropriate district-level administrator to obtain information. You may also review an *Operational Guidelines* document from another district and conduct an analysis.

b. Assume you are the superintendent of Good Luck ISD. As superintendent, describe the way you plan to communicate with the board to be sure the board is aware of issues before the district and to ensure that the entire board has a complete understanding of any issue on which they are likely to be asked to decide. In addition, describe your plans for communication with the board during times of crisis.

c. Review the board's most recent operating procedures or guidelines for board behavior. If your board has no such document, review a similar document from another board. Write a critical analysis of the board's procedures or guidelines and suggest additions or changes that you would like to see enacted in your board's operating procedures.

d. Identify and describe state and local requirements for school board member training. How and by whom are required training requirements monitored? Are there additional training requirements for the board president/chair? Are board member training requirements different for experienced board members? Visit the website for your state's school board association. What types training are offered through that organization?

e. Develop a presentation intended for the governing board which reviews the annual goals. Include an advocacy statement which will enable the board to support policies and programs that promote equitable opportunities and success for all students of differing socioeconomic background, ethnicity, gender, or disability.

f. Identify a current contentious issue between constituency groups or individuals within the district. Develop a plan which includes regular communications with the community about their concerns and how to advocate for the district's position.

g. Other related activities assigned or approved by your district supervisor and/or program advisor, or activities that are part of a larger project.

NELP Standard Component 7.2

Understand and demonstrate the capacity to design, implement, cultivate, and evaluate effective and collaborative systems for district governance that engage multiple and diverse stakeholder groups, including school and district personnel, families, community stakeholders, and board members. The superintendent candidate should be able to:

♦ Evaluate district governance and stakeholder engagement systems.
♦ Design governance systems that engage multiple and diverse stakeholder groups.
♦ Implement strategies (i.e., communication) that support stakeholder engagement in district governance.
♦ Cultivate and coordinate an effective and collaborative system for district governance.

Discussion:

In todays' society school district constituents want transparency in leadership decision-making and an opportunity for input before decisions are made. Diverse stakeholders wish to share ideas, not only at board meetings, but during the development of policy and program restructuring. The superintendent should develop a systemic approach to provide those opportunities. District websites, newsletters, and social media posts are examples of how districts are communicating with stakeholders. School districts will vary in their communication strategies based upon the uniqueness of the district and those interested in governance of the district. What strategies are proving to be effective in your school district?

   It is highly recommended that interns select activity a) as one of their chosen activities to demonstrate this skill component.

Choose activities below that you desire to include in the initial internship plan to meet the expectations of this national standard component. The district supervisor may adapt some activities or replace with other activities that meet this standard component. The majority of the activities are recommended for maximum learning and experience.

a. Review current district policy for governing unscheduled speakers at board meetings. Summarize the current process for a patron who wishes to speak before the board and consider whether you would like to see changes or adjustments in the process. After summarizing the current process, make an argument for keeping the current process as it currently is or suggest changes that you believe would enhance communication with the board. Be sure to justify your position.

b. Study board policy and procedures documents to determine whether the board maintains standing committees and if committees consist of other district employees and/or parents and patrons. If so, share your opinion regarding this governance model. If your district does not implement such a model, conduct some research to determine if there are better strategies to involve and engage patrons, parents, and employees in the governance model. Share examples of how you believe that parents, patrons, and employees could be more involved and engaged in district governance. Limit your commentary to two pages or less.

c. Review the composition and structure of your school district board of trustees. Is the structure of the board comprised of single-member districts, positions voted at-large, or is the board structure comprised of both single-member and at-large positions? Write a paper describing the structure in your school district and share your opinion whether the current structure assists or hinders board member diversity.

d. Interview three current or former superintendents to determine their expectations in the development of a positive, respectful, and responsive relationship between board members and leadership. How does each sustain this positive relation?

e. Compare the process used in your school district to develop and approve the school district calendar to the process used by two other school districts of your choosing. Are there differences in the way the calendar is developed and approved? Is there shared input from multiple stakeholders in the process? Identify the process that you believe is best and explain your position.

f. Other related activities assigned or approved by your district supervisor and/or program advisor, or activities that are part of a larger project.

NELP Standard Component 7.3

Understand and demonstrate the capacity to evaluate, engage in decision-making around, implement, and appropriately communicate about district, state, and national policies, laws, rules, and regulations. The superintendent candidate should be able to:

♦   Evaluate the implications of educational policy for district practices.
♦   Develop a plan for the implementation of laws, rights, policies, and regulations.
♦   Communicate about district, state, and national policy, laws, rules, and regulations.
♦   Coordinate decisions and district policies with policies and/or regulations from local, state, and federal policy entities.

Discussion:

School district superintendents make decisions that are often controversial. It would be great if most decisions were "win-win" situations. But the truth is most decisions will be supported by some constituents and disliked by others. Communicating influential elements that affect decisions is important, especially if the influential elements are requirements of policy, laws, rules, and regulations that neither the superintendent nor district control. Providing patrons information before a decision is made is often referred to as transparency. It is easier to provide guiding information before the decision is made than to explain why the decision was made afterwards. How will you prepare for difficult decisions when the time comes?

It is highly recommended that interns select activity a) as one of their chosen activities to demonstrate this skill component.

Choose activities below that you desire to include in the initial internship plan to meet the expectations of this national standard component. The district supervisor may adapt some activities or replace with other activities that meet this standard component. The majority of the activities are recommended for maximum learning and experience.

a. Review governing board policy or current practice to determine how your district receives legal advice. Answer the following questions in your investigation:
    1. Does your district pay an attorney an annual or semi-annual retainer fee to provide advice when needed?
    2. Does your district pay an attorney an hourly fee to provide advice only when needed?
    3. Does the board require their attorney to be present at board meetings?
    4. Does your district depend on legal service through a law firm that specializes in school law?
    5. Who has access to the district's legal advisor? (Is it only the superintendent or do other administrators have access to the district's legal advisor?)
    Based on the answers to these questions, make suggestions on strategies that you will consider as superintendent that you believe will provide the district with adequate legal advice and protection at a reasonable cost to the district.

b. Review your district policy manual. Look specifically at the file identification information that is likely to be found at the top or bottom of each page of the manual. Look to see what information is provided. One may expect to see information such as the date that this specific policy was enacted or approved and whether the policy is a local policy or a policy derived from state or federal law. What is the process the district governing board utilizes to revise and update policies? How often do revisions and updates occur?

c. Describe the efforts of your school district to communicate board policy to employees, students, and community members regarding educational law, health and safety requirements, and state agency guidelines that influence the programs and practices of the school district. What additional district communication efforts would you recommend?

d. Visit appropriate regional, state, and national organizations' websites that primarily represent school board members, i.e., National School Board Association and state school board association. What are the current issues or topics addressed and how might your school district would be impacted by those positions? What benefits are derived from membership and participation, i.e., conferences, newsletters/journals, training, networking, etc.? Is there a requirement for board membership? What limitations are there on membership and travel paid by the district? Review the most recently approved budget for your school district and determine the total amount of funds allocated for board training and travel. What recommendations would you make for the level of involvement and participation of board members in these organizations?

e. Meet with a member of the district leadership team to review any district, state, and/or federal policies which challenge current district operations. In what ways do any policy present a challenge to the district and make recommendations for resolving the challenge.

f. Other related activities assigned or approved by your district supervisor and/or program advisor, or activities that are part of a larger project.

NELP Standard Component 7.4

Understand the implications of larger cultural, social, economic, legal, and political interests, changes, and expectations and demonstrate the capacity to evaluate and represent district needs and priorities within larger policy conversations and advocate for district needs and priorities at the local, state, and national level. The superintendent candidate should be able to:

♦ Use evidence to evaluate district needs and priorities vis-à-vis education policy conversations and emerging challenges.

♦ Represent the district and its priorities and needs at the local, state, and national level.

♦ Advocate for the needs and priorities of the district at the local, state, and national level.

Discussion:

It is important that the superintendent be an advocate for the school district and an excellent communicator. To be both, the superintendent must be proactive and initiate conversations with appropriate individuals associated with local, state, and national organizations and/or government entities. People in government and those who have influence with organizations and the larger community cannot help your school district if they do not know the needs of the district. What additional skills do you need to become an advocate for your district's needs?

It is highly recommended that interns select activity a) as one of their chosen activities to demonstrate this skill component.

Choose activities below that you desire to include in the initial internship plan to meet the expectations of this national standard component. The district supervisor may adapt some activities or replace with other activities that meet this standard component. The majority of the activities are recommended for maximum learning and experience.

a. Meet with the superintendent or other respected school leader knowledgeable of the history of the district. Identify the organizations, agencies, and political/civic groups in your community that have relationships and influence with the school district. How will you address philosophical and political differences between board members and between the board and outside stakeholders?

b. Identify three current social trends or emerging challenges which are impacting student learning outcomes. Prepare a one-page white paper which address one emerging challenge which left unchecked, will negatively impact the district.

c. Ask the superintendent to share ways that he/she attempts to represent the district and/or advocate for the best interests of students in the district. Summarize what you learn from the superintendent and reflect on the best strategies to achieve this goal.

d. Identify three strategies for closing the achievement gap between minority student achievement and that of white students. Propose strategies which could work in your district, but which are not currently utilized.

e. Review laws, rules, regulations, and policies and then collect and use data to compare the effectiveness of program(s) or processes in place in the district such as special education, gifted and talented program, and athletics. Prepare and present a report describing your findings and/or make recommendations for improvement.

f. Other related activities assigned or approved by your district supervisor and/or program advisor, or activities that are part of a larger project.

2.2 Foundational Leadership Skill Activities

This section provides a brief overview of 12 essential competencies for leadership development. It is intended to provide a frame of reference for the intern to practice, reflect, and assess skill development. It is assumed that the intern has previous instruction and more in-depth study in each of these areas. Following each competency overview, a list of analysis questions is provided. Use these to analyze current performance and the development of future actions to address current problems encountered and assist in alleviating similar problems in the future. The 12 competencies are:

1. Developing Trusting Relationships.
2. Leading in the Realization of the Vision.
3. Making Quality Decisions.
4. Communicating Effectively.
5. Resolving Conflict and Issues.
6. Motivating and Developing Others.
7. Managing Group Processes.
8. Supporting Others with Appropriate Leadership Style.
9. Using Power Ethically.
10. Creating and Managing a Positive Culture and Climate.
11. Initiating Change.
12. Evaluating student, personnel, and program performance.

When problems occur or needs arise, people tend to focus on the immediate crisis. This focus may alleviate the current need but does little to ensure that organizational learning has occurred, or similar problems will occur less often. In these situations, leaders find themselves endlessly putting out the same types of fires. Consideration of each of the 12 competencies gives the leader the bigger picture and the necessary information to guide future actions for organizational improvement, heightened quality of life within the organization, increased learning, and the opportunity for developing self and others. To gather the necessary information, the leader must ask the right questions to determine if competencies are needing development and improvement. The analysis questions provide for a more comprehensive definition of the problem and thus allow for more appropriate action. With enough practice, this framework of thinking becomes second nature to the leader.

1. Developing Trusting Relationships

Covey (2009) believes there is one thing common to every individual and organization and that if removed, will destroy the best of organizations. He adds that if it is developed, it can bring unparalleled success. That one thing is trust. Green (2011) further noted that trust affects every relationship in your life and determines whether one realizes their dreams. He believes that without trust, true success is impossible. Trust is found in many books on leadership to be crucial for success in leadership, if not the base of all leadership success.

Having confidence in the leader's honesty and ability has a great impact on the climate, culture, communications, and overall quality of life within the organization. Distrust breeds negativity, erases motivation, and is a major cause of turnover. Interns and new leaders must face the challenge of developing trusting relationships. Trust is not given with title or pay scale but must be earned. Trusting relationships and positive outcomes are impacted when empathy is evident, especially when used in considering the opinions of others. When leaders emphasize empathy people demonstrate a willingness to be more innovative and engaged. Also, employees with leaders demonstrating empathy reported a more inclusive workplace (Brower, 2021). This takes time and a determined effort to prove to others your reliability, honesty, and character. It can take years to earn trust but can be erased in a moment. The wise leader understands this and begins to take actions to build and sustain trust. These actions include being honest in every dealing with others, following through with commitments, admitting mistakes, and knowing their strengths and limitations. They also initiate ways to truly know others and let others truly know them. They believe in individual worth and see individuals teaching versus simply faculty and staff. They view themselves as individuals leading versus a title or role and give credit to others when deserved, practice active listening and take feedback seriously, invest time in relationships, focus on nonverbal communications, and put their trust in others (Ahmed, 2020).

Being oneself does not require a role. Interns face broken relationships with other teachers as they move into administration. New relationships must be formed, and new trust developed. Future school leaders must utilize research, practice, reflect, and form habits of developing and sustaining trusting relationships.

Analysis Questions for Trust

To What Extent:

♦   Has trust through competence, honesty, and follow-through been established?
♦   Has the leader relied upon/trusted others?
♦   Is transparent leadership modeled in the school?

What actions need to be taken to address any concerns from above to solve the current problem and avoid similar problems in the future?

---

2.   Leading in the Realization of the Vision

A clear vision is the cornerstone of teams that function in harmony (Bambrick-Santoyo and Lemov, 2018). Vision is one aspect that the research has long held to separate leaders from administrators or managers. The administrative manager is one that "copes with complexity" or manages the current status quo, while the leader is "coping with" and initiating change (Kotter, 1998). Thus, mangers are concerned with the efficiency of the current system, while leaders look for greater effectiveness with new policies, procedures, and systems. Once the leader is in touch with the real concerns of the employees, they can connect them to the vision rather than chasing revisions to the vision statement (Nawaz, 2021).

It is difficult to lead in schools today with many teachers and parents fearful of and resistant to change. It is equally difficult to lead the district or school when only those elected have the power to change. Additionally, beginning district leaders attempt to do things right and fulfill their job descriptions; they begin to behave like managers, not leaders. Realizing the vision involves risk and it is critical that district goals and vision are communicated to campus and department leaders so that the various entities within the district align with the district (Mombourquette, C., 2017).

Leaders strive to move the organization and all its members to a new vision. Reducing risk and increasing the possibility of success for the vision requires all the other 11 competencies. The vision and the means to get there require understanding, effort, and support from the entire organization. They do not have to create the vision by themselves but are responsible for providing the leadership for vision creation, articulation, and support. Future leaders must utilize research, practice, reflect, and form habits of developing and working toward the realization of the vision.

Analysis Questions for Vision

To What Extent:

♦ Is there a clear vision of how the organization should be functioning now and in the future? Is it shared by all?
♦ Is the mission of the organization appropriate, understood, and supported?
♦ Has adequate planning and discussion occurred?
♦ Are the vision, mission, and plans aligned with the key principles and beliefs of those in the organization?
♦ Is the vision a broad-based, comprehensive picture of the processes, interactions, and accomplishments of all relevant stakeholders, i.e., students, teachers, parents, and administrations?

What actions need to be taken to address any concerns from above to solve the current problem and avoid similar problems in the future?

---

3. Making Shared Decisions

Decision-making is crucial to educational administration because the school, like all formal organizations, is basically a decision-making structure (Hoy and Miskel, 2001). Decision-making is a process that guides actions. Decisions are based on one's beliefs, values, and previous experiences. Leaders must know themselves; know why they choose particular paths; know who to involve; and know which decision-making model to use.

Judgment plays a critical role in making good decisions. Seeking relevant data from a variety of sources, analyzing information available to identify important elements, evaluating data sources for relevance and reliability and establishing criteria for evaluating the effectiveness of a decision are all crucial elements in making effective shared decisions.

A person making decisions without utilizing these factors often makes bad decisions quickly.

It is assumed that the intern has deliberated on their key beliefs or principles and has some degree of understanding of the similarities and differences between themselves and others. He/she should continue to use reflection to make decisions: reflection will help the intern more fully understand the roots of their beliefs and the impact of those beliefs on decisions. This section will briefly review levels of involvement in shared decision-making.

Educational leadership has come a long way since the scientific management era in the early twentieth century. Then, the ones at the top made the decisions and believed that a rational model would shape optimal decisions. They believed they could know all alternatives and predict the results of each alternative. Today, we know better. We know that those at the top cannot accurately gather or predict all alternatives. We know that followers deserve to be involved and better decisions are made with input and collaboration. The first decision is to decide what level of involvement is most effective.

Leaders have at least four options of involvement in decisions: deciding alone, seeking participation and input, seeking collaboration, and letting others decide. The wise leader uses participative and collaborative strategies for all-important decisions. However, this cannot always be done, nor should it always be done. The leader must assess five factors to decide on the level of involvement of others:

1. Time. Urgency may require the leader to decide for him/herself. Participative and collaborative decisions require more time. If important decisions need more involvement, the leader must schedule additional time for greater involvement.
2. Staff interest in the decision. People differ in the things that interest them and the level of interest. For leaders desiring more participation or collaboration, interest in the decision must first be generated.
3. Expertise of the staff. At very low levels of expertise, followers typically accept the decisions of the leader and would have little to contribute. Leaders that desire greater collaboration, however, must raise levels of expertise to successfully involve subordinates.
4. Importance or need for a high-quality decision. Some decisions are much more important and carry significant consequences. This is almost always the case for instruction and learning, whether directly or indirectly. For important questions that demand a high-quality decision, greater participation or collaboration is needed.
5. Degree of need for buy-in or support for the decision. Many decisions in schools need the support of the staff for successful implementation and results. A collaborative model most often increases buy-in and support.

We live in a time of empowerment and involvement in decisions. The wise leader understands that better decisions are made with higher levels of involvement. This leader also understands that involvement does not simply happen or is always the best approach. Greater involvement and a collaborative (shared) decision model take time to plan, and it takes effort to educate and motivate staff to participate effectively. The resulting better decisions are worth the effort.

Analysis Questions for Decision Making

To What Extent:

- ♦ Was the appropriate decision-making model used?
- ♦ Were the major steps in decision-making followed?
- ♦ Was the appropriate level of involvement used?
- ♦ Were those affected by the decision included in the process?

What actions need to be taken to address any concerns from above to solve the current problem and avoid similar problems in the future?

4. Communicating Effectively

"Without exception, all major national school administration associations in this country stress the importance of effective communication skills" (Gorton and Snowden, 2002, p. 31). Although leaders spend countless hours communicating with others, effective communication is a challenging task. Communication has the power to bring individuals and communities together or create division and getting it right is imperative (Lewitter, et al., 2019). Despite this imperative, schools are generally criticized for poor communication between leaders and faculty, teachers and other teachers, faculty and students, and school and community.

What do we know about communication? First, it is impossible for one person to imagine a concept or event, find the words or actions to describe (encode) it, relay these words or actions (transmit), and make another person understand (decode) the message exactly the way it was originally imagined. The difficulty of transmitting feelings, impressions, and related experiences unique to every individual only magnifies this dilemma. It is the leader's responsibility to continuously work toward more effective communication and better understanding among all individuals.

Secondly, we know that there are four major communication skill areas. The first is that leaders must be proficient in giving information. This includes oral, written, and technological information (email, web pages, Excel, Power Point, Zoom, Web-Ex, etc.). Oral communication skill is a critically judged aspect of a leaders' performance. Leaders are judged on many verbal attributes including, voice, volume, tone, rate of speech, use of pauses, avoidance of speech crutches, i.e., "uh", "you know", mastery of audio-visual equipment and technology. Writing skill is equally important because of the volume of writing a leader performs. Spelling and correct grammar and contextual usage are crucial factors in communicating. Leaders must be highly proficient in the second area of communication: listening and receiving information. These two aspects of communication involve verbal and nonverbal strategies and cues. The successful leader develops both effective verbal and nonverbal behaviors.

In considering both giving and receiving information, a leader should emphasize receiving information. Covey (1989) found that successful leaders seek to understand before they seek to be understood. Listening and receiving information first allows the leader to have the whole picture, as opposed to giving information and allowing only others to know both sides and perspectives. Carnegie (1993) teaches that no one is more persuasive than a good listener. Listening results in many other positive outcomes. These include:

- Shows interest and respect for others.
- Allows others to vent and models appropriate social skill.
- Increases learning and understanding of other perspectives.
- Critical for resolution of conflict.
- Forms the habit and appearance of wisdom.
- Allows time for observing others' information, e.g., body language, inflection, emotion, etc.
- Allows time for listening to what your mind, heart, emotion, and body are telling you.
- Builds rapport and meaningful relationships.
- Develops a culture of open communication.

The third aspect of effective communication is the design and management of a communication system. Ultimately, the leader is responsible for communications within the organization and outside the organization. Without an effective system, the leader must depend on others for the accuracy and amount of information. This is often less than adequate because:

- Others often tell leaders only what they believe the leader wants to hear.
- Others may tell the leader only the positive side.
- Others may tell the leader only the negative side.
- Others often omit vital information.
- Many do not communicate with the leader.

An effective communication system involves a variety of formats and avenues of communication. Successful leaders may regularly use meetings, surveys, interviews, group processes, suggestion boxes, needs assessments, open-door policies, the practice of walking the halls, eating in the cafeteria, and a host of others. The goal is to have enough means of communicating that allow different people to choose the format that they like and are willing to give and receive information. The breadth of avenues and formats also allow the leader to give and receive diverse types of communication.

The fourth and final aspect of communication is monitoring and evaluation of the first three, i.e., giving, receiving, and the system. Leaders must periodically evaluate the quantity and quality of the communication within the organization, as well as outside the organization. Future leaders must utilize research, practice, reflect, and form habits of effective communication.

Analysis Questions for Communication

To What Extent:

- Did others infer my intended meaning?
- Have I fully understood what others are trying to say?
- Are people utilizing differing avenues of communication?
- Have I reached my entire intended audience?
- Is there a safe and open system for communication?

What actions need to be taken to address any concerns from above to solve the current problem and avoid similar problems in the future?

5.   Resolving Conflict and Issues

Conflict is inevitable and should warn the leader that a problem exists. Although unique situations may warrant different practices, the ideal approach is to problem-solve collaboratively. Thomas (1976) identified five styles of managing conflict: competing, collaborating, compromising, avoiding, and accommodating. Competing is similar to a directive style, where a directive must be given, regardless of the competing belief. Compromising works well in the short-term, but it usually does not totally resolve the conflict. Accommodating is necessary when the leader is wrong or simply willing to give in to the other side. Avoiding is seldom recommended, except for buying time for things to "cool off" or gather additional information. The collaborating style uses problem-solving strategies and is the most often recommended style.

"Disagree and Commit" is a management tactic used by Jeff Bezos, as it encourages faster decision making. Conflict can slow or impede making needed decisions. Bezos believes that failures are acceptable, however slow decisions are not. This tactic promotes healthy disagreements and celebrates risk-taking (Adams, 2021). However, in self-assessments conducted in graduate leadership classes, the authors of this text found that most students initially avoided conflict. To the novice, this makes perfect sense – who wants to be in a conflict? However, the wise leader views every conflict as an opportunity to improve the organizational effectiveness, improve the quality of life for some or all its members, and an opportunity to better know and understand each other.

The two major areas of conflict facing leaders are conflict over differing expectations of roles and differing beliefs that, if not resolved, become issues. Role conflict can take the form of the classic model developed by Getzels (1968), where the personal needs of individuals conflict with the needs/expectations of the organization. These conflicts arise in numerous and varied ways. For example, the school may expect a teacher to work with others in a group or team-teach, while the teacher prefers to work alone. Conflict usually occurs when individuals believe that another is acting outside of his role or not fulfilling the expectations of the role. One might hear "He is not supposed to do that" or "She is not doing her job". It is imperative that the leader and followers have a mutual understanding of the expectations of the various roles within the school. Both job descriptions and performance evaluations must be aligned and conform to the agreed-upon expectations of the role.

Issue resolution is another competency essential to leadership. Issues develop out of differing opinions or beliefs on a host of topics, such as policy, practice, goals, the means for reaching goals, values, etc. The wise leader welcomes issues and views them as an opportunity for improvement and better understanding of all parties. As with role conflict, problem solving approaches work best. Typically, the leader seeks consensus on the goals of either side of an issue and ensures both sides fully understand the opposing position. The leader then solicits all concerns and attempts to find a different and better solution that either side proposes. In this manner, when one side is in favor of Plan A and their opposing side is either in favor of Plan B or simply against Plan A, the leader seeks a Plan C. Self-restraint, patience, composure, and humility have emerged as major leadership characteristics needed (Jit, et al. 2016) Leaders must utilize the research on conflict resolution and then practice, reflect, and form habits of resolving conflict and issues.

Analysis Questions for Conflict and Issue Resolution

To What Extent:

- ♦ Do all persons within the organization understand the duties and responsibilities of his or her position and the positions of others?
- ♦ Are expectations for others realistic and aligned with job descriptions?
- ♦ Is conflict seen as an opportunity?
- ♦ Have steps been taken to resolve personal conflict and/or issue conflict? Have steps moved both sides toward a different and better solution?

What actions need to be taken to address any concerns from above to solve the current problem and avoid similar problems in the future?

---

6.   Motivating and Developing Others

No human venture succeeds without strongly motivated men and women (Gardner, 1993). The wise leader understands that there is no universal motivation for every individual but seeks to discover what motivates the people that he/she leads. There are many theories on motivation, and each may be partly true for some people.

There is a deep tradition of behavioral thinking in public schools. For all practical purposes, behavioral theories are not accepted or used by most psychologists. The field has moved past Pavlov and Skinner, who believed that the key to increasing motivation is to provide consistent and appropriate consequences to reinforce desired behaviors. Alfie Kohn (1993) challenged the reliance on rewards to motivate individuals with his provocative book *Punished by Rewards*. He contends that hundreds of studies have shown that rewards produce only temporary compliance and that no lasting change in attitudes or behaviors can be attributed to the use of rewards. Control over others and the manipulation of reality is inappropriate and unethical. Unfortunately, many school leaders wonder, "What rewards and punishments can we use to induce others to act appropriately?" Leaders need to move from behavioral perspectives to cognitive motivation and learning theory and practice.

Successful superintendents build capacity in others by modeling interactive communication, converting conversations into action by requiring the use of data, and advancing professional accountability by building habits of self-reflection (Giannini, 2021). The intern must be knowledgeable of motivation theory and attempt to increase motivation for improvement. The key is to understand what motivates (or inspires) each member of the organization. Future leaders must utilize research, practice, and reflection to develop traits that motivate those they lead.

Analysis Questions for Motivation

To What Extent:

- ♦ Are the needs of the people being met?
- ♦ Are the needs of the people in line with the needs or the organization?

> ◆ Are differing processes used to motivate? Are they effective?
> ◆ Are varying methods used to develop others?
>
> What actions need to be taken to address any concerns from above to solve the current problem and avoid similar problems in the future?

7. Managing Group Processes

Warren Bennis (2000) believes that our world is the product of "Great Groups", teams of creative persons who banded together to achieve remarkable successes that would not have been possible through a traditional hierarchical approach. The traditional school, however, is a place where work is done individually.

Breaking with this tradition and reforming the culture where faculty and administrators collaboratively work toward school improvement requires commitment to empowerment, developing new leaders, cooperation, and shared responsibility. Leaders must invest time, effort, and expertise to overcome traditions, past failures, and lack of interest and/or expertise on the part of faculty (and administrators) to work together. Overcoming prior negative attitudes is a difficult, but not impossible task. It is the responsibility of the leader to provide new positive experiences in working in groups with shared goals, shared responsibility, shared authority, and shared decision-making.

Calling in the entire faculty to announce what could have been put in writing is insulting and a waste of time. Likewise, calling a meeting to discuss failures of a few faculty members wastes the time of all others. The need to meet should be common sense. Meeting involves discussion, learning, group thinking, and group work. Obviously, a leader should develop a set of principles or rules for meetings and use effective skills in conducting the meeting.

The following is an example of rules for meetings:

- ◆ Schedule meetings only when necessary and a need to meet. Information that can be put in writing should be communicated through email, memos, or other means of two-way communication between meetings.
- ◆ Prior to the meeting, distribute an agenda with purpose, time, and location listed. Participants in meetings should come prepared and know that they have a say in their meetings and that their input is valued.
- ◆ Meetings should be arranged and organized for participation. The leader may use a circle or semicircle or at least stand or sit on the same level.
- ◆ The leader should solicit participation from and show interest in individual members. He/she should model listening skills and value the comments and conflicting perspectives from the members.
- ◆ The leader should stay on time and on task. Often, leaders plan for more than can be accomplished at one meeting. Thus, time management is vital, and the leader is responsible for keeping to the item or task at hand.
- ◆ The leader summarizes accomplishments of the meeting and follows up on decisions. Followers quickly lose respect and trust in leaders that speak well but do not follow up. Followers expect meetings to produce results. Follow-up is crucial in establishing a culture where meetings are viewed as important and productive.

Faculty members meet at other times than in leader-called meetings. This may be grade level or subject area department meetings, committees, task forces, or a host of other types of groups. If the leader expects these meetings to be productive, training must be given. Members need guidelines, adequate information, clear understanding of purposes and goals, and they learn to work in a group. These groups may have an assigned leader, such as the department chair, or the task may be assigned, and a leader may emerge. Productive groups do not just happen. They must be developed.

To overcome many negative attitudes of meetings, committees, and working groups, the leader must truly believe in others and their abilities to accomplish tasks and make effective decisions. It is imperative that future school leaders utilize research, practice, reflect, and form habits of effective group processes to solicit support, develop new leaders, and reach organizational goals.

Analysis Questions for Group Processes

To What Extent:

♦ Have the formal and informal groups been identified?
♦ Are all groups working productively and collaboratively?
♦ Are goals for the groups realistic, understood, and acceptable?
♦ Is trust and freedom of expression the norm of all groups?
♦ Are meetings used effectively and efficiently?

What actions need to be taken to address any concerns from above to solve the current problem and avoid similar problems in the future?

---

8. Supporting Others with Appropriate Leadership Style

For decades, researchers have studied leadership style. They have coined many terms to describe leadership styles. Goleman (2000) devised six terms that describe various styles used by business leaders: coercive, commanding, affiliative, democratic, pacesetting, and coaching. He found coercive and pacesetting to be negative and the other four to be positive. For our purposes here, we will use the following six terms of styles to consider for appropriate use:

1. Directive. Often described as authoritative, autocratic, or commanding, this style is used when strict compliance is needed, or it is an emergency or urgent situation. The directive style is appropriate for quick changes or guidance. It is also appropriate when only the leader has the necessary knowledge or expertise.
2. Participative. Often labeled democratic, this style is used when limited time is available and/or the leader holds most of the accountability for the results. With this style, the leader makes the final decision or approves policy or practice but gathers input from others. Ideally, this involves all those affected by the decision or action.
3. Collaborative. Also labeled democratic, this is the ideal style and is a means of working in true collaboration with others. This style values others' expertise and helps develop future leaders. This style requires adequate time, training, and a shared responsibility. In most cases, better decisions are made with the use of a collaborative style.

4. Coaching. The leader remains in a leader/mentor/teacher role with the subordinate. This is also an ideal style when followers are not prepared for true collaboration. Coaching frees the subordinate to practice as a leader, while remaining under the guidance and assistance of the formal leader.

5. Affiliative. This style is appropriate when the leader has more concern for the person or persons than the task. This could be when trying to build positive relationships or persons are dealing with personal issues. Once the personal problem has passed or the relationship has been formed, the leader can focus on the task and use a coaching or collaborative style. It should be noted that this is opposite of Goleman's pacesetting style where the task takes precedence over people.

6. Laissez-Faire. This style is seldom recommended but may be appropriate for minor tasks where followers have more expertise and interest than the leader.

The key to using the most effective style is to know the situation and people and strive to meet the needs of both. In some cases, the entire staff must be dealt with using a very directive style and at other times, only some of the staff needs a directive style. In some cases, some of the staff needs coaching, while others are at a level of collaboration. The main lesson is that people and situations, not the leader's preferences, dictate what style the leader should use.

Analysis Question for Leadership Style

To What Extent:

♦ Was the appropriate style used with differing people and/or in differing circumstances?

What actions need to be taken to address any concerns from above to solve the current problem and avoid similar problems in the future?

---

9. Using Power Ethically

A leader must wield power to accomplish great things. Although many believe power corrupts or no person should have power over another, power can be both positive and negative. The wise leader understands the negative potential of power but strives to use power for good. In the classic model of power, French and Raven (1959) believe there are five basic types of power: reward, coercive, legitimate, referent, and expert.

The use of reward power is tempting. Many believe it is right to reward others for their effort and feel a sense of joy in giving to those that deserve it. However, the use of reward power can do more harm than good. In giving rewards to some, others are overlooked. In giving rewards, some begin to expect it and may only work for reward or limit their efforts to the criteria set for the reward. Additionally, it is impossible to find a reward that everyone is willing to work for. The reward system becomes a "game", and many get tired of playing. The result is that the leader's power is diminished. Use of reward power is not recommended.

Coercive power is an obvious misuse of power. Yet, coercive power is often used with students. Making threats to children for misbehavior or poor academic performance carries over to administration, and threats are then made to faculty and staff. The use of coercive power is unethical. Coercion and punishment do not solve problems in schools. The wise leader refrains from using either reward or coercive power.

Legitimate power is derived from the authority given to the position. Superintendents have authority over principals; principals have authority over teachers; and teachers have authority over students. Depending on the history and culture of the district, however, the power given to a position may vary. Some teachers have very little power over students and some principals exert minimal power over the faculty. It is others that give power to the leader, so is he/she cannot depend solely on the power of the position. The wise leader understands both the powers inherent to the position and the powers not given to the position.

Referent power is the ideal. Followers give power to leaders that they identify with, believe in, and trust. To increase referent power, the leader must know others and allow them to know him or her. The leader must work with others, find consensus in the vision, and determine the means of achieving the vision. Gaining referent power requires effective communication and a strong belief in the value of others and working together.

Expert power comes from possessing special knowledge or skill. Followers freely give power to experts for help and guidance. To increase expert power, the leader must commit time and effort to become more expert in essential areas of leadership and education.

The wise leader understands that empowering others in the quest for school improvement builds a broad power base. If one gives out power, he/she gains power. Only in politics would one view this as giving up power. Empowering others builds support, buy-in, consensus, and the development of current and future leaders. It is imperative that future school leaders utilize research, practice, reflect, and form habits of using appropriate style and power to reach organizational goals and positively and ethically meet the needs of everyone they lead.

Analysis Questions for Power

To What Extent:

- Has the leader exerted the appropriate use of referent or expert power?
- Has the leader exerted the misuse of coercive or reward power?
- Is delegation of duties and power given in the organization?
- Do faculty, students, and parents feel empowered?

What actions need to be taken to address any concerns from above to solve the current problem and avoid similar problems in the future?

---

10. Creating and Managing a Positive Culture and Climate

The only thing of real importance that leaders do is to create and manage culture (Schein, 2010). This is best understood when one considers that the school's vision, ways of making decisions and communicating, amount and type of conflict, degree of motivation, use of power, and the ability to change are all ingredients of the culture. The culture also includes the history, traditions, and beliefs of the organization, and the relative importance of each. People form attitudes toward the values, norms, expectations, and practices that set their school apart from others (Greenberg and Baron, 1997).

Leaders are responsible for understanding the culture, promoting a more positive culture, and taking actions that create a climate or environment in which great ideas can happen (Sinek, 2011). They realize that culture changes over time and that subcultures exist. Cultural changes need a shared commitment and require extensive follow-up for the change to become an accepted aspect of the new culture.

The culture of a school or school district is critically important in helping students and families who are struggling with circumstances that make academic and emotional progress difficult. For example, given the recent influx of undocumented immigrants across the southern border of the country, many schools will be facing unprecedented challenges in their efforts to assimilate and help students, many of whom are separated from parents and many with significant gaps in their formal education and a large percentage of whom are suffering from post-traumatic-stress disorder. In addition, many of these students find themselves in legal limbo as they wait for immigration judges to decide whether they can stay or will be deported. Language barriers often complicate every step of the process. Indeed, in many districts, English language learners, many of whom are recent immigrants, are the fastest growing segment of the student population. Most schools are not equipped and entirely overwhelmed and unable to deal with the social-emotional problems of these students and know that they need to feel safe and comfortable before learning can take place (Mitchell, 2015).

Another area in which the culture of a school or school district plays a critical role is in preparing students for a career or work. There is currently underway a big national push to include much stronger workforce connections in K-12 by revamping curriculum and school culture to help students explore potential careers – including some that their teachers, principals, and district leaders can't even imagine yet (Klein, 2020). William "Kit" Moran, the principal at Dexter High School near Dearborn, Michigan said, "In a perfect world, getting ready for postsecondary and career would be the same thing" (Klein, 2020). However, in the community in which Mr. Moran serves, there is a compelling expectation in the community and among parents that all students are prepared to succeed in a competitive university regardless of their skills or aptitude. Many educators complain that they are expected to tie curriculum tightly to standardized tests which makes it very difficult to devote time and focus to the soft skills that students will need in the workplace such as: communication, collaboration, critical thinking, and creativity (Klein, 2020). Paul Newton, the principal at Westfield Middle School in Massachusetts says, "There is a lot of pressure on kids to do well on standardized testing and so the first thing that suffers are all of these employability skills" (Klein, 2020). A school district culture and climate which recognizes the need to prepare students for success in future work and technology opportunities as well as in postsecondary education contributes not only to the well-being of its students, but also to the health and welfare of future societies.

The school district leader should also be aware of the climate and act if the current climate is negative in nature. School climate is simply defined as the feelings or atmosphere of the school. Climate can change quickly and often. The task of creating and maintaining a positive, nurturing climate in a school district has become more of a daunting challenge in recent months. According to Stephen Sawchuk, superintendents and school boards are suddenly being asked to balance conceptual debates over issues such as race, equity, and individual rights with the real obligations of allocating and spending significant amounts of cash. School boards have traditionally been the loci of intense cultural debates. Debates over evolution, offensive mascots, and loyalty oaths have surfaced in the school environment in the past. However, in recent years, issues which have polarized the nation have provoked school boards and school patrons across the nation (Sawchuk, 2021).

Consequently, the school district leader must be proactive in dealing with climate. The leader can use formal assessments, develop trusting relationships, have effective means for communicating, and seek to know the feelings and atmosphere daily. Leaders should be very sensitive to staff and student morale and take responsibility for the well-being of sanguinity in the district. The superintendent should investigate the causes for low morale and implement plans and actions designed to foster assurance and confidence within the district.

Climate and culture are extremely important aspects for measuring the quality of life in the school. Quality of life affects academic performance, behavior, staff turnover, motivation, health, and the mental health of all members of the school. Future leaders must utilize research, to evaluate district practices, reflect on those practices, and form habits of assessing, improving, and creating a positive school culture and climate.

Analysis Questions for Culture and Climate

To What Extent:

♦ Have adequate assessments been conducted to assess the culture and climate?
♦ Are there concerns with the current school culture or climate and if so, have adequate time and resources been allocated for needed improvement?

What actions need to be taken to address any concerns from above to solve the current problem and avoid similar problems in the future?

---

11. Initiating Change

Successful leaders initiate and manage change. Of all the skills presented in this text, leading change is the most difficult. Initiating change and leading change is such a challenge because it requires individuals to confront and move beyond one's previously held beliefs, values, and assumptions. Nick Polyak, a superintendent in the Chicago area, says, "We as human beings are really good at learning new things, but we're really bad at unlearning things that are no longer true" (Will, 2019). Margaret Goldberg describes the change paradox in this statement: "I think that's one of the reasons that leading something like this is really difficult", she said. "Partly you need buy-in and partly you need changes to happen fast for kids because they have one shot at 1st grade. But on the other hand, adult learners need longer than one school year to learn, grow, and change" (Will, 2019).

Michael Fullan (2001) asserts that there are two main aspects of educational change: what changes to implement (theories of education) and how to implement change (theories of change). They interact and shape each other, but the critical factor is the distinctiveness of the individual setting. What works in one setting may not work in another.

What do we know about change?

♦ It is a process that takes place over time (two to three years).
♦ The process has steps or stages and requires a change in belief.
♦ It must begin with the individual, then out to organization.
♦ It is difficult, seldom worth the effort, and most changes fail.

♦ A real need or pressure is required and not everyone will change.
♦ No amount of information will make the change totally clear.
♦ It will always have disagreement and conflict.
♦ The leader has a key role in facilitating.
♦ Those affected by change must be involved in the process.
♦ It must be evaluated and monitored from beginning to end.
♦ Improvement cannot occur without it.

The most startling aspect cited in the list above is that most change efforts fail. Most experts recommend attempting only one or two changes at a time. The wise leader must fully understand the change process and choose their change efforts wisely. Most people fear and/or resist change. Change causes disequilibrium in individuals and they seek the balance of the past.

What are the factors in resistance to change?

♦ Some agree with new programs but never do anything.
♦ Some need more time – they rationalize resistance.
♦ Some are against any change made from a state or national level.
♦ Some only rely on costs – is it worth the time and effort?
♦ Some only want incremental change and fear large change efforts.
♦ Some are successful and are very conservative toward change.
♦ Some lack the skill to make the change or have an honest difference of opinion.

Leaders can take appropriate actions to reduce resistance despite these factors. These include:

♦ Allow teachers to feel the change is their own.
♦ Show that the change reduces rather than increases their burdens.
♦ Involve others and reach consensus on the value of the change…
♦ Validate and recognize objections and give feedback and clarification.
♦ Develop support, trust, and confidence with those involved.
♦ Set attainable and realistic goals and be open to revision and improvement.
♦ Change and resistance to change are inevitable: the leader must guide and direct it.

Factors for successful change efforts:

♦ Broad-based ownership – including informal and formal power.
♦ Positive relationships have been built.
♦ Support from administration and community awareness.
♦ Fits philosophy, mission, and culture of school.
♦ Has a moral purpose and is relevant to those affected by the change?
♦ Planning, evaluation, and adequate resources are available.
♦ Monitoring and adjustment in process occur.
♦ More training occurs during implementation than at first.
♦ Few, if any, other big changes are occurring at the same time.

These lists were compiled from the works of Robert Evans (1996); Hendricks and Ludeman (1996); Peter Senge et al. (1999); Tony Wagner et al. (2006); Hall and Hord (2001); and Michael Fullan (2001). It should be noted that the lack of any one variable might cause the change to fail.

It has been said that change is the only constant in life. It has also been said that everyone wants improvement, but no one wants change. The skill of effecting change is one that requires much thought, analysis, and effort. Despite the hurdles, if one is to lead, one must lead change. Future leaders must utilize research, practice, reflect, and form habits of leading educational change.

Analysis Questions for Change

To What Extent:

- Is the change proposed only one of a few?
- Is there a moral purpose in the new change?
- Do all involved understand the change process?
- Have positive relationships been built?
- Is the creation and sharing of information a priority?
- Has a productive disturbance and a subsequent coherence been accomplished?
- Have steps been taken to reduce resistance?
- Have the factors that produce success been implemented?

What actions need to be taken to address any concerns from above to solve the current problem and avoid similar problems in the future?

---

12.   Evaluating Student, Personnel, and Program Performance

A significant portion of educational policy space is occupied by the various evaluation systems which are intended to enhance accountability and support school development. In recent decades, the practice of evaluation and related activities such as auditing, inspection, and performance measurement have grown exponentially. The institution of education is one of the most densely populated social sectors in terms of evaluation, monitoring, and accountability (Lindgren, 2016). Some researchers have identified a paradigm shift in the organization of evaluation from an event done by an expert at a single point in time to a mandatory, repeated, and routine system of appraisal often done by organizations or institutions (Lindgren, 2016). Since this fundamental shift has occurred, educational evaluation has often evolved into an emphasis on standards, data, indicators, and benchmarks or, as some have described it, "governance by numbers" (Lindgren, 2016). Such a shift has also enabled public and private stakeholders to utilize publicly available statistics and data to create their own evaluation plan or rating system.

It is interesting to note that teacher evaluation came under intense scrutiny more than a decade earlier. As a result of this scrutiny, researchers found that annual teacher evaluations were traditionally based on information from a single source: observations from principals (Loewus, 2017). Consequently, in 2009, more than two dozen states stiffened their teacher evaluation requirements. In 2009, the New Teacher Project published a report known as "The Widget Effect" in which findings indicated that 99% of all teachers were being rated as "satisfactory" (Loewus, 2017). Based on this finding, policymakers and education leaders began questioning the validity of evaluation systems that failed to distinguish among teachers. In the same year, the Obama Administration began its "Race to the Top" program. The "Race to the Top" program offered states financial incentives to include student test data in their evaluation systems.

In 2011, the United States Department of Education began offering states relief from some of the stringent requirements in federal education law by offering waivers. Among other provisions, the law mandated that all students perform at grade level in reading and math by 2014. In order to gain the flexibility which they sought, states had to commit to linking student achievement outcomes to their teacher evaluation systems. With so many incentives in place, the number of states using student growth data in their evaluation of teachers and schools skyrocketed. At the end of 2009, 15 states included student performance outcomes in their evaluation systems. By the end of 2015, 43 states included such data in the evaluation system (Loewus, 2017). However, with the passage of ESSA in 2015, the governance of teacher evaluation programs was essentially placed back in the hands of the states, in essence renouncing the Obama administration's push for strict test-based accountability (Loewus, 2017). Today, some of those policies requiring the use of student data for evaluation purposes are still in place. However, some states have begun reversing mandates on using student growth measures and standardized test scores, for the purpose of assessing teacher and school quality.

While teacher evaluation and personnel evaluation require much of the attention and energy of school district administrators, there are a plethora of evaluations and evaluation systems in which school districts are engaged. The list below provides a summary of some of the evaluations which may afford guidance and information for the superintendent. The topic of evaluation is complex, controversial, and involves many entities, subjects, criteria, and beliefs. The federal government, unions, accrediting agencies, boards of education, universities, real estate agencies, the press, and a host of professional organizations all rate and evaluate public schools. If anything is worth doing, it is worth evaluating and finding improvements. Only through meaningful, valid, and reliable evaluation can strengths, weaknesses, conflicting efforts, and wasteful efforts be identified to allow leaders to analyze and take appropriate actions. Ratings and labeling do little to find answers. Evaluation must be thorough and have adequate breadth and depth to be meaningful and useful.

Evaluations should be administered on the following:

♦ Faculty, staff, and students.
♦ Recruiting, hiring, staff development, and retention.
♦ Programs and cocurricular activities.
♦ Curriculum, instruction, and testing.
♦ Technology.
♦ Community and parent relations.
♦ Food service, transportation, facilities, and safety.
♦ Fiscal accountability and legal compliance.
♦ All 12 Leadership competencies.

This list is not exhaustive, but it does show the scope of what needs evaluation. Only through evaluative information can leaders plan appropriate action for improvement. The evaluation must begin with the existing practice and measure the extent of progress toward the vision or final goal. Beginning, formative, and summative measures should be taken at appropriate intervals. Care must be taken to choose evaluative instruments that reliably measure what you intend to measure. It is highly recommended that a future leader study and develop new skills in the use of evaluative data to increase learning and the overall performance of the school.

Analysis Questions for Evaluation

To What Extent:

- ◆ Are effective personnel and program evaluations established?
- ◆ Are both formative and summative evaluations utilized?
- ◆ Is data from evaluations used for decisions and planning?

What actions need to be taken to address any concerns from above to solve the current problem and avoid similar problems in the future?

Activities That Can Be Embedded Under the Foundational Skills Theme

During the internship, you will encounter issues concerns, or conflicts. Analyze the issue by addressing the analysis questions under each of the 12 foundational skills above. Choose one or two of the 12 foundational skills in which you feel that you need additional expertise. Focus on improving the skill over time. Document your goals and activities and reflect on key learning. Following meeting your first skill development goals, choose another foundational skill and repeat the process. Continue the process until all skills needing additional practice and expertise have been addressed. Your goals, and reflections will be included in the final internship report.

2.3   District Service Activities

The internship plan should balance the needs of the intern and the needs of the district. The final plan should not be centered selfishly on your development, nor should you limit your experience by submitting totally to the specific needs or concerns of the district. Care must be taken, however, that a realistic balance is maintained. Activities not in the text or assigned by the preparation program are designated as service activities. Service activities will come mainly from the district supervisor's recommendations. They can be written in the "Other" category listed under any of the NELP standard components where there is a logical fit. These may be assistance on current needs and projects, assistance with day-to-day administrative duties, or other needs that the district supervisor believes will benefit the district. In almost all cases, service activities will also benefit the intern. The intern MAY NOT log more than eight hours on any one chosen activity unless it is a longer-term project. The intent is to ensure an adequate breadth of experience and not limit the internship with repetitious activities after adequate experience was gained. Normal or routine duties of the intern's current position may not be counted as internship hours.

2.4   Independent Leading Activities

The intern is required to take an independent leadership position in at least one intern activity and more than one is preferable. This requires leading other adults. The activity should be directly related to the district goals and related to the improvement of student performance.

Typically, leading a longer-term activity or project is assigned by the district supervisor. Discuss options with your supervisor and keep in mind that being allowed to take an independent leadership role may not be approved until the intern has established the trust of the supervisor or circumstance for leading a project have surfaced. Interns are typically never given complete independence but if allowed a high degree of decision-making, it is considered independent leading. The activity must:

♦ Include other faculty or staff in a group process.
♦ Be led by the intern.
♦ Have a plan that includes:
   1. Need for the activity.
   2. Goal of the activity.
   3. Resources available.
   4. Timeline.
   5. Method of evaluation.
♦ Include foundational skills used (e.g., decision-making and communication.)
♦ Be approved by the district supervisor.

The intern may choose a large activity or several smaller activities. It is strongly recommended that the size and number of leading activities be considered with respect to time needed to fulfill other activities and current job responsibilities. The intern is strongly advised to accept a leadership role in as many activities as can reasonably be accomplished.

References

Adams, G., Seven ways I'm learning to "disagree and commit". *Transformation Solutions*, (n.d.). Retrieved November 2, 2021: https://mytransformationsolutions.com/disagree-and-commit/.

Ahmed, Anam (2020). How to Maintain and Develop Trust in Work Relationships. Retrieved from: https://smallbusiness.chron.com/develop-maintain-trust-work-relationships-12065.html

Bambrick-Santoyo, P., & Lemov, D. (2018). *Leverage leadership 2.0: A practical guide to building exceptional schools* (2nd ed.). San Francisco: Jossey-Bass.

Bennis, W. (2000). *Managing the dream*. Cambridge, MA: Perseus Publishing.

Brower, Tracy (2021). Empathy Is the Most Important Leadership Skill According To Research Retrieved from: www.forbes.com/sites/tracybrower/2021/09/19/empathy-is-the-most-important-leadership-skill-according-to-research/?sh=6a1b4ce43dc5

Carnegie, D. (1993). *The leader in you*. New York: Simon & Schuster.

Covey, S. R. (1989). *The seven habits of highly effective people*. New York: Free Press Publishing.

Covey, S. R. (2009). *The speed of trust: Live from L.A.* New York: Covey.

Evans, Robert. (1996). *The human side of school change*. San Francisco: Jossey-Bass.

French, J. R., & Raven, B. (1959). The bases for social power. In D. Cartwright (Ed.), *Studies of social power* (pp. 150–167). Ann Arbor: University of Michigan Press.

Fullan, M. (2001). *The new meaning of educational change* (3rd ed.). New York: Teachers College Press.

Gardner, J. (1993). *On leadership*. New York: Simon & Schuster.

Getzels, J. W. (1968). *Administration as a social process*. New York: Harper & Row.

Giannini, A. L., *Strategies Superintendents Use to Build Leadership Capacity with Executive Teams*, (2021). Dissertations. https://digitalcommons.umassglobal.edu/edd_dissertations/388

Goleman, D. (2000, March–April). Leadership that gets results. Brighton, MA: *Harvard Business Review*, 78–90.

Gorton, R. A., & Snowden, P. E. (2002). *School leadership and administration* (6th ed.). New York: McGraw-Hill.

Green, A. (2011). *Beyond wealth*. Hoboken, N.J.: John Wiley & Sons, Inc.

Greenberg, J., & Baron, R. A. (1997). *Behavior in organizations* (6th ed.). Englewood Cliffs, NJ: Prentice Hall.

Hall, G. E., & Hord, S. M. (2001), *Implementing change: Patterns, principles, and potholes*. Boston: Allyn and Bacon

Hendricks, Gay, & Ludeman, Kate. (1996). *The corporate mystic: A guidebook for visionaries with their feet on the ground*. New York: Bantam Books.

Hoy, W. K., & Miskel, C. G. (2001). *Educational administration: Theory, research, and practice* (6th ed.). New York: McGraw-Hill.

Jit, R., Sharma, C. S., & Kawatra, M. (2016), Servant leadership and conflict resolution: A qualitative study. *International Journal of Conflict Management*, 27(4), 591–612. https://doi.org/10.1108/IJCMA-12-2015-0086

Klein, A. (2020). Data: 5 big challenges in preparing K-12 students for the world of work: Schools are trying to forge stronger workforce connections in K-12 by revamping curriculum and school culture to help students explore potential careers. *Education Week*, 39(20), 3. Retrieved November 2, 2021, from: https://libproxy.lamar.edu/login?url=https://www.proquest.com/trade-journals/data-5-big-challenges-preparing-k-12-students/docview/2355127743/se-2?accountid=7043

Kohn, A. (1993). *Punished by rewards*. Boston: Houghton Mifflin.

Kotter, J. P. (1998). What Leaders Really Do. *Harvard Business Review on Leadership*. Boston: Harvard Business School Press.

Lewitter F, Bourne P. E., & Attwood T. K. (2019), Ten simple rules for avoiding and resolving conflicts with your colleagues. *PLOS Computational Biology* 15(1), e1006708. https://doi.org/10.1371/journal.pcbi.1006708

Lindgren, L. H. (2016, September). Evaluation systems in a crowded policy space: Implications for local school governance. *Education Inquiry*, 7(3), 237–258. https://dx.doi.org/10.3402/edui.v7.30202

Loewus, L. (2017, November). Are states changing course on teacher evaluation?: Test score growth plays lesser role in six states. *Education Week*, 37(13), 1. Retrieved November 3, 2021, from: https://eds-p-ebscohost-com.libproxy.lamar.edu/eds/detail/detail?vid=2&sid=0382e022-02c9-42c4-bc9e-d9f0d4e5ff4d%40redis&bdata=JnNpdGU9ZWRzLWxpdmU%3d#db=edsgac&AN=edsgac.A515815343

Mitchell, C. (2015). Undocumented students strive to adapt: Some schools help youths get foothold in language, culture. *Education Week*, 34(29), 3. Retrieved November 2, 2021, from: https://libproxy.lamar.edu/login?url=https://www.proquest.com/trade-journals/undocumented-students-strive-adapt/docview/1681270896/se-2?accountid=7043

Mombourquette, C. (2017). The role of vision in effective school leadership. *International Studies in Educational Administration*, 45(1), 19–37.

Nawaz, Sabrina (2021). 5 Reasons why your employees don't understand your company's vision. *Change Management*. Retrieved from: www.hbr.org/2021/09/5-reasons-your-employees-dont-understand-your-companys-vision

Sawchuk, S. (2021, July 29). https://www.edweek.org. Retrieved from *Education Week:* https://www.edweek.org/leadership/why-school-boards-are-now-hot-spots-for-nasty-politics/2021/07

Schein, E. H. (2010). *Organizational culture and leadership* (4th ed.). San Francisco: Jossey-Bass.

Senge, P., Kleiner, A., Roberts, C., Ross, R., Roth, G., & Smith, B. (1999). *The dance of change: The challenges of sustaining momentum in learning organizations.* New York: Currency Doubleday.

Sinek, S. (2011) *Start with why.* London: Penguin Books.

Thomas, K. (1976). Conflict and conflict management. In M. D. Dunnette (Ed.), *Handbook of industrial and organizational psychology* (pp. 889–936). Chicago: Rand McNally.

Wagner, T., Kegan, R., Lahey, L., Lemons, R. W., Garnier, J., Helsing, R., & Rasussen, H. T. (2006). *Change leadership: A practical guide for transforming our schools.* San Francisco, CA: Jossey-Bass.

Will, M. (2019). We as human beings are really good at learning new things, but we're really bad at unlearning things that are no longer true. *Education Week*, 38(33), 7. Retrieved November 3, 2021, from Education Week: https://libproxy.lamar.edu/login?url=https://www.proquest.com/trade-journals/whats-harder-than-learning-unlearning/docview/2229806394/se-2?accountid=7043

Internship Plan Implementation

Following final approval of the plan developed in Stage 2, the intern can begin implementing leadership activities. This stage describes further how the intern can seek assistance in meeting requirements of the internship experience.

3.1 Collaboration with District Supervisor/ Roles and Responsibilities

After completing Stage 1 and making preliminary choices of activities in the seven NELP Standards and foundational leadership skills, the intern should meet with the district supervisor to reach consensus on a plan for the internship. The intern and district supervisor should discuss district needs and priorities and the intern's preferred activities and decide the nature of the service activities and the local project(s) described in Sections 2.3 and 2.4. The plan should provide adequate breadth and depth of activity in each of the professional standards to assess progress toward mastery and independent leadership.

Roles and Responsibilities
Preparing Effective District Leaders

The role of the superintendent is complex and requires a broad range of knowledge and skills. According to Darling-Hammond et al. (2007), the quality education that aspiring leaders receive in their preparation programs and a sustained effort on continuous growth after they are hired is a factor in whether they can meet the high expectations for the position. Educator preparation programs should be delivered to best meet the needs of adult learners and to allow administrative interns to apply their learning in authentic settings with a focus on real-world problems and dilemmas (Darling-Hammond et al., 2007). This can be accomplished with internships/practicums that require the application of acquired skills, knowledge, and problem-solving strategies within school settings. Kolb et al. (2001) found that real-world practice increased a leader's ability to think about, examine, and systematically plan strategies for school improvement. Ideally, strong educator preparation programs provide interns with an intense internship/practicum that provides them with opportunities to be a part of the day-to-day operations of the school environment under the supervision of an expert mentor. In addition, educator preparation programs should provide the intern ample time to reflect on the activities and how those activities informed their future role as a school leader.

DOI: 10.4324/9781003299493-4

For the internship experience to aid in the development of effective district leaders, the field-based experiences need to be more than passively observing district leaders or attending meetings. The experiences should have sufficient breadth. The activities should give interns opportunities to demonstrate that they have the knowledge and skills to manage organizational change, create significant learning environments, lead a district improvement initiative, communicate, and work collaboratively with all stakeholders, and build capacity within the organization. The experiences should also enable interns to advance to independently lead activities (as outlined in Stage 1). Good mentors are the key component of educator preparation programs designed to equip interns for continuous school improvement. To develop the knowledge and skills to successfully demonstrate the intern's proficiencies, a district supervisor is critical for providing guidance to interns.

The Intern

Each intern is responsible for completing their required internship hours and for developing, participating in, documenting, and reflecting on their internship experiences throughout the program. Intern responsibilities include the following:

- Discuss the internship scope and responsibilities and how to initiate the internship with the university/program advisor prior to beginning.
- Draft an initial Internship Plan including activities to meet national standards and individual leadership knowledge and skill needs.
- Initiate a meeting with the district supervisor to discuss the internship scope and responsibilities and the needs and goals of the district.
- Obtain approval of the internship plan from the district supervisor and program advisor.
- Engage in all tasks and responsibilities outlined in the plan, while being available for leadership development opportunities throughout the internship.
- Maintain a log and reflective journal on all internship activities.
- Meet regularly with district supervisor and program advisor throughout the internship to discuss observations and hands-on learning experiences, gain feedback on internship responsibilities and work, and be assessed on leadership knowledge and skills.
- Produce internship documentation, reflections, and reports as required by the university/program officials.

All interns are expected to demonstrate professional conduct and integrity throughout the entire internship experience and program. They are to keep sensitive information confidential, take initiative in guiding his or her internship experience, maintain clear communication with their district supervisor and university/program advisor, and generally behave in a professional manner.

How challenging your internship experience will be, to a great extent, is up to the intern. Like the adage "You get out of it what you put into it", interns are urged to raise the bar and seek a true challenge for several very important reasons. First, the intern will be observed during their experience and others will clearly see the rigor and expectations that were planned. Second, while being an intern, there may be no other time when so many leaders will take the time to teach, counsel, and assist in the learning, development, and practice. Third, the day will come when interns are standing in front of a group of very bright, educated, and experienced adults "expecting" to see a confident and competent leader. The internship is the opportunity to build the confidence and competence for that day. Interns will meet and learn from a wide variety of individuals such as the personnel director, athletic director, principal, superintendent, board member, and parents and leaders in the community. Their reputation can move from a skilled and competent teacher or building-level leader to a skilled and competent district leader. And finally, throughout a leadership career, one can positively affect the lives of thousands of students.

Program Advisor

The program advisor provides collegial and individual support to his or her assigned intern throughout the internship. The advisor facilitates ongoing reflection of the intern's experiences that addresses specific actions taken and deeper consideration of the assumptions and values that they bring to these roles, as well as of their personal leadership styles, practices, and the ways that values, style, and practices are intertwined:

- The advisor helps to develop each intern's plan at the beginning of the internship.
- The advisor helps to identify potential projects or significant work-related assignments to meet the NELP or other standards-based performance assessment expectations for program completion or licensure. These are to be included in the proposed plan, detailing the requirements, scope, and products, and expected assessment-related expectations.
- The advisor meets formally with each intern either one-on-one, in small groups (such as conference groups) or in whole group seminars throughout the internship period. During these sessions, the advisor encourages intern reflection on the leadership role and work, facilitates discussions of internship challenges and leadership strategies, and fosters leadership development generally.
- The advisor meets with each intern on-site periodically throughout the internship. During the on-site visits, the advisor observes the intern in their work and consults with the district supervisor to ensure that the internship experiences are varied and appropriate and are in keeping with the intern's internship plan. The advisor provides written or oral feedback to the intern.
- The advisor monitors each intern's field experiences using the logs and reflective journal. The advisor should evaluate the breadth and depth of the intern's work, using the NELP standards or other standards as a framework in reviewing their hours. The advisor should also evaluate the completed projects using the same standards and assessment rubrics. Using this information, the advisor can provide regular feedback and guidance as appropriate.
- The advisor meets regularly with the intern and internship supervisor to discuss the internship content, the intern's leadership opportunities for independent work, address problems and challenges, and identify new learning priorities.
- The advisor reviews the intern's progress in completing any required performance tasks, using standards-based expectations.
- The advisor is available to the intern and internship supervisor by phone and email for problem solving and guidance.
- The advisor provides the intern evaluative feedback at the end of the internship experience.

District Supervisor

The district internship supervisor is typically the intern's superintendent or assistant superintendent. He or she assigns the internship work, supervises the intern, and coordinates the intern's work. The district internship supervisor functions as a role model, supervisor, coach, and mentor throughout the intern's experience. The supervisor guides the intern, challenging him or her to grow as educational decision maker, instructional leader, and manager of a complex organization.

The district internship supervisor should have a demonstrated record of effective educational leadership, particularly as outlined by the NELP standards; have the time and interest to supervise the intern throughout the internship period; and be committed to the program's vision of educational leadership and their role in developing quality leadership in interns. The internship supervisor should help the intern plan out projects to be completed as part of the internship, supporting the intern in garnering resources and undertaking the work to be done. Finally, the district internship supervisor should support a developmental approach to mentoring the intern, from providing exposure and orientation to promoting independence and responsibility. The district internship supervisor's responsibilities include the following:

- Meet with the intern initially to discuss the internship scope and the intern's responsibilities throughout the internship.
- Meet with the intern regularly (at least weekly) to discuss their responsibilities, progress, and leadership learning experiences, as well as to provide guidance and assistance in helping the intern and providing feedback as needed.
- Provide the intern with exposure to various district-level leadership experiences.
- Provide the intern with developmental leadership experiences, with graduated responsibility and leadership.
- Identify possible performance tasks or projects that the intern can complete to meet NELP performance assessment expectations; provide support for the intern's work.
- Orient the intern to district leadership as a career and provide coaching on the job search and interview process as well as advice on transitioning from teaching to leading careers.
- Meet with the intern and program advisor intermittently to review the intern's progress and discuss the internship experience.
- Provide formal feedback and assessment of the intern's work and leadership development at the end of the internship.

As advice for internship supervisors, we offer the following recommended mentoring practices:

- Offer new challenges. Be mindful of interns' strengths and encourage them to take on responsibilities that are "outside of their comfort zone".
- Provide wide exposure. Provide exposure to a wide range of leadership experiences through shadowing and co-participation at meetings inside and outside the district. Couple shadowing and co-participation with reflective conversations.
- Enable buddying. Create an informal buddy system and foster networking by pairing the intern with another new administrator.

♦ Meet weekly. Schedule a weekly time to meet with the intern (i.e., first thing in the morning or end of the day on Friday) to debrief on the week's experiences, internship experiences, and other matters. Hold this time as "sacred".

♦ Provide exposure to the practice of other leaders. Expose interns to other leadership styles in and outside the district and follow up with reflective conversations about situational leadership and differences in approaches.

♦ Enable performance task completion. Assist interns in completing program-required or other performance tasks that enable the interns to demonstrate their leadership skills and accomplishments.

♦ Provide presentation opportunities. Arrange for interns to make small and large group presentations such as at a faculty meeting, committee meeting, PTA meeting, or board of education meeting.

♦ Confidentially discuss personal matters. Use personnel and student matters (while respecting confidentiality) as mini-case studies for talk-aloud problem solving and reflection.

♦ Be aware of how interns are presented publicly so that other staff will take their contributions seriously.

♦ Demonstrate balance. Encourage discussion about the whole person, so interns can explore issues of work, family, and career balance.

♦ Use interns as a resource. Take advantage of opportunities to engage interns in supporting the implementation of initiatives and evaluation of gaps or differences in utilization.

♦ Facilitate transition. Review interns' existing school and district responsibilities and redirect their work as appropriate (particularly to wind down prior-existing committee work and to take up new responsibilities).

♦ Enable group process facilitation. Give interns more opportunities to work with various groups, so they can learn more about multiple needs and perspectives, and how to balance them.

3.2 Interviewing

It is highly recommended that the intern schedule interviews with various key district and community leaders in the early part of the internship. Although this will occur after your initial internship plan is approved, new information and feedback from interviewees may offer interns alternative and/or additional activities to consider in improving and modifying the initial approved plan. Interviews, however, should be only a small part of the overall experience. Most of the time should be spent working as opposed to observing or listening. Interviewing can affect several key outcomes that the intern should consider. These include:

♦ Meeting the right people and developing a network of experienced district leaders.
♦ Knowing the various leadership positions and their responsibilities.
♦ Providing the opportunity for current leaders to get to know you.
♦ Forming new relationships – administrator to intern administrator, versus administrator to teacher/other.
♦ Understanding different departments and perceptions from leaders and followers within each department.

♦ Insights into additional or more relevant internship activities.
♦ Getting the "bigger picture" and having experienced mentors provide answers to questions/concerns from various areas and perspectives.

Interview questions:

1. Tell me about your department/area.
2. Tell me about your job duties and responsibilities.
3. What are your goals?
4. What are your present major concerns?
5. What future concerns are anticipated?
6. What have you done to improve this district's capacity to better meet the needs of students?
7. What do you need, expect, or hope for from the superintendent?
8. From your experience, what advice would you give a new superintendent?
9. **What activities would you suggest I undertake during my internship to better understand and/or work with your department/area?**

Add any additional questions appropriate to your knowledge and skill experience need.

The following list is recommended persons to interview. Smaller districts may not have persons holding these titles and may fall under the superintendent's responsibility or another designated employee.

♦ Curriculum Director
♦ Chief Financial Officer
♦ Personnel Director
♦ Technology Director
♦ Transportation Director
♦ Food Services Director
♦ Maintenance Director
♦ Public Relations Officer
♦ Board Member (with permission of the superintendent)

3.3 Networking

Professional networking is defined as an individual's attempt to develop and maintain relationships with others who have the potential to assist them in their work or career and is an important tool for success (Baumann & Utz, 2021). As a candidate in your superintendent preparation program, you share common interests with others in the program. When you share professional information with each other you are networking. Successful leaders use networks to seek advisement, discuss ideas, and improve their ability to fulfill the responsibilities of their positions. According to Porter and Woo (2015), decision-making, work performance, career development, and job search are primary motivators These networks often consist of mentors, peers, experts in various fields, community leaders, friends, and colleagues from professional and civic organizations. The internship offers the opportunity to meet and develop professional relationships with key school, district, and community leaders. These people in your professional network may assist in the internship and be available later in your career. It is recommended that you plan to interview, meet, or work with key people.

Effective networks may be developed in both an online environment and through personal, live interaction. Superintendents who seek networking opportunities in a face-to-face environment will often join local, regional, state, and national professional organizations. Most professional organizations meet on a regular basis and provide venues for members to share information, hear presentations about contemporary topics, and provide written materials of interest to members. Some professional organizations will provide a mentor to new superintendents for the purpose of helping when guidance is needed. Meetings and conferences provide opportunities for formal interaction as well as informal networking. It is not unusual to hear a conference attendee state, "the conference presentations were good, but I also learned a lot by participating in the hallway discussions".

A potential benefit often associated with networking opportunities via personal contact is confidentiality. There are times, however, when we do not want everyone to know "what we don't know". Identifying a colleague or mentor that you trust and value his or her opinion can be valuable in terms of professional networking. Seek individuals that have the expertise and are trustworthy. They may offer great opportunities for networking.

Candidates within your superintendent certification program constitute a network. Some of your colleagues will soon be hired as superintendents and they will be looking for talented individuals to fill key central office positions. Will they be familiar with your personal and professional traits, skill sets, knowledge, and ability to work as a team member and consider you as a prospect for any central office position that might be needed? As you progress through your certification program, you are making an impression with your college professors, instructors, and your fellow candidates. You want those impressions to be good.

Scholars have shown that networking is an important career self-management strategy associated with career success (Spurk, Hirschi, & Dries, 2019). LinkedIn is the most popular professional social networking site (Totoro, 2017) with over 660 million users in 200 countries (LinkedIn, 2019). However, studies have been conducted that recognize the value of contemporary social networking sites, particularly when identifying career opportunities. Knowing that a position in a nearby school district is coming available before the position is posted can be of significant benefit to someone interested in the position.

Social networking sites also offer the opportunity for users with similar interests to develop a "closed network for designated users" that offers greater confidentiality than an "open" network site. An example of this professional networking opportunity would be superintendents of school districts in the same county sharing information about bad weather and coming to consensus about school closures. Sharing information about the number of individuals sick and the possibility of closing schools is another example where sharing information would be beneficial. The issues generating the need to share information will change with time, but the need to share confidential information is continuous.

Professional organizations often provide information by utilizing online newsletters or group email to members. Often the communication will contain links to other sources of information, such as legislative action, state education decisions, etc. This type of information reserved for members of professional organizations constitutes added value to those who have made the decision to join a network provided by professional organizations. These opportunities to learn are benefits derived from your willingness to participate in professional networking.

3.4   Reflective Practice – Log and/or Journal

The intern must meet with the university/program advisor and agree on the method of documenting the internship experience. Typically, logs should cite date, time (rounded to the half-hour), a brief statement describing the activity, and the state or national standard met. An example:

Date	Time	Description of Activity	Standard
9/05/22	8.0 hour(s)	Served on district professional development committee.	

Many internship programs require a reflective statement following each log entry. The advantage to this is that interns must reflect immediately following the entry into the log. Other programs separate the journal and summative log with a requirement of a more in-depth journal entry. The intern should meet with the university/program advisor and collaboratively decide on the method that best meets the needs of the intern and program.

We highly recommend that interns maintain a journal about their internship experiences, for documentation, note taking, and reflection "The brain does its best reflective work when provided with the time, place, and tools for the deliberate exercise of reasoning skills" (Dickmann & Stanford-Blair, 2002, p. 206). Benefits of journaling have been identified as: expanding awareness, understanding, and insights; making connections between theory and practice; and generating new hypotheses for action. Interns should keep a reflective journal of their building-level internship experiences, as a companion to their logs. Through these, interns can reflect on the significance of their internship activities for personal growth and achievement of district goals. The reflective journal is also a means for recording and examining practical and ethical dilemmas. The reflections should relate experiences to the professional standards.

Journaling assists the emerging leader in focusing on essential leadership skill, knowledge, and needed disposition. Journaling also provides an opportunity to reflect on results of the intern's efforts. The reflections should raise ideas about how an intern might alter or improve an activity as a district leader in the future, and show evidence of reflective skills in application, analysis, synthesis, and evaluation. Time and thought used in journal writing reinforce the learning and assist in the leader's ability to truly begin reflection prior, during, and after action. Interns often keep journal entries in a separate file on the computer, while others prefer handwritten formats. The type of journal you keep is your choice unless required otherwise by the university. Interns may find that journal entries help in compiling the final report. What is key is being systematic in when and how a journal is kept and the process of review, analysis, and reflection. It is recommended that an intern complete at least two journal entries per week. Other typical journal formats and reflective practices are:

- Daily (5–10 minutes) – Many try journaling daily for a two- to three-week period and then reflect on patterns found following this period.
- Weekly (30–45 minutes) – Many try journaling weekly for one month and then reflect on patterns found following this period.
- Intermittent – Many make journal entries following significant insights, feelings, and/or experiences.
- Projects – Many interns keep a journal while leading major projects and reflect on the leadership experience and results.

Guiding or key questions to assist in reflecting upon and evaluating entries are:

♦ What are you learning about your leadership style, strengths, and/or development areas?

♦ What belief, experience, or disposition caused a particular judgment?

♦ Did you notice any personal feelings, e.g., stress, frustration, tired, or happy, warm relationships, etc.? What do you believe was the cause?

♦ How did you arrive at a decision made? Did you consider other alternatives? Why was your choice the best one?

♦ What are you learning about diversity (for example, but not limited to, race, culture, and language diversity, diversity of thought, diversity of educational approach). Did you react differently to some students, peers, or supervisors? If so, why?

♦ What challenging leadership situations or leadership opportunities have you experienced and how have you addressed them? What did you learn and how might you address the situation or opportunity differently as a leader?

♦ What examples of best practice have you observed and in what area, and how might you build upon those practices in your own leadership work?

♦ Did you observe any change in knowledge, skill, or disposition?

♦ How were your actions conducive to increased learning, district improvement, and/or development of self and others?

♦ How did your experience provide progress on mastery of specific state and/or national standards?

Reflection is an important learning strategy in leadership development. By stepping back and reflecting upon what was learned, what worked or did not work, and how course readings, experiences and other theory and research might inform the work, candidates gain insight into understanding the nature of district leadership and their own leadership skill development and proficiency. Reflection with supervisors and peers is critical to one's self-development and is an essential practice for effective problem-solving. Reflective journals are submitted to the university/program advisor, and NOT to the district supervisor. This is because some journal entries may be negative about the district supervisor's words or actions.

3.5 Use of Data

School leaders use a wide variety data throughout the breadth and depth of their leadership work (Bernhardt, 2006; Bernhardt, 2015; Militello et al., 2009). They must become accustomed to creating systems and routines for the validity and reliability of the evidence they collect and use, including creating consistent practices for collecting data and valid criteria for what is collected and how it is used. Increasingly, school leaders use data to make better decisions, foster thoughtful problem solving, and engage others in continuous improvement (Bryk et al., 2015; Forman et al., 2017; Schildkamp et al., 2019). Thus, they need systems and routines around regular, thoughtful data review and use in these ways that productively involve and develop others as data-informed problem solvers.

Unlike many other professions, school leaders use a variety of data, often in combination, to set direction, engage in problem solving, and monitor and evaluate results. By triangulating a variety of data sources – such as resources, student performance, and staff evaluations – school leaders can pinpoint opportunities for improvement or gaps and needs to be addressed. Moreover, such triangulation can be used further to investigate and address issues of disproportionality in student discipline and special education referrals that may be causing inequities by race/ethnicity and gender (Fergus, 2016). As an intern, you must be mindful of how school leaders in your internship setting use multiple sources of data for problem solving and identify ways in which such use could be improve.

As an intern, you have an opportunity to make use of a variety of school-related data in undertaking your leadership preparation experiences. Some data you will collect yourself – interviews with school leaders and staff, observations of activities, and solicitation of input and feedback. This will provide you with an opportunity to practice designing, collecting, and using data for improvement purposes. Other data you will compile from existing sources, whereby you will have an opportunity learn how to use these data for variety of purposes – improvement planning, accountability, evaluation, and problem solving. Throughout the planning section (Stage 2) of this text are a variety of data-related activities that will enable you to practice collecting and using a wide variety of data sources and types across the standards areas that frame your leadership work.

You are strongly urged to seek out opportunities to learn about these data sources, their use and limitations, and means of using them collectively as part of continuous school improvement. Throughout, you are also strongly urged to demonstrate your proficiency in using various data collection, analysis, and display tools, such as Qualtrics or SurveyMonkey for survey research, Excel for information management, analysis and display, SPSS for statistical analyses, and PowerPoint for information sharing and reporting.

1. Pay attention to the culture of data use in the school (Gannon-Slater et al., 2017; Lasater et al., 2020):
   - What data are available?
   - How are data used in planning, implementation, monitoring, and evaluation of related work?
   - Who has access to data?
   - Who uses data regularly and how?
   - What are commonly investigated questions, particularly as related to equity or disproportionality?
   - How are data-related reports shared within the school community? Within the broader community and public-at large?
2. Throughout your internship experience, be mindful of the breadth and depth of data you use and the tools for which you gain proficiency (Bernhardt, 2015). Document the extent to which you have exposure to and gain proficiency in using:
   - Student and staff demographic data.
   - Student behavior and academic performance data.
   - Student, teacher, and community feedback survey data about the school culture and climate.
   - Teacher and staff feedback surveys about professional development or implementation of new curriculum, programs, or procedures.
   - Budgetary data.
   - School performance report.
3. As part of one or more projects or assessment tasks, try to combine two or more sources of data in planning, implementation, and analysis of the work and your accomplishments, noting these explicitly in your documentation.

3.6   Intern Information/Documentation Management

Be sure to check with your preparation program advisor to determine whether a portfolio or other means of evidence documenting their knowledge, skills, and accomplishments is required. It is important to have a system to store documentation of internship activities, work products, assignments, and accomplishments for analysis, reflection, and reporting purposes. Preparation programs often organize internship documentation according to meeting state and/or national standards, or specific program requirements. It is highly recommended that interns update documentation weekly to include log, journal, reflections, and work products.

3.7   Monitoring and Adjusting the Internship

Plans typically need to be changed. Changes occur because of:

- ◆ Unexpected events (fires, floods, hurricanes, pandemics, school shootings, etc.).
- ◆ New opportunities that arise.
- ◆ Suggestions/recommendations from mentors and/or interviewees.
- ◆ New perspectives gained from experience and reflection.
- ◆ Results of periodic formative evaluations.

Any or all the above can arise and cause the intern to adjust, add, and/or delete planned activities. The intern should determine and schedule periodic assessment of their progress and plan. Formative evaluation should be completed monthly or more often, if needed. This should be a combination of self-evaluation and supervisor observation. It is recommended that after self-evaluation on progress and accomplishments, the intern meet with their district supervisor and collaboratively discuss the quality and quantity of intern activities undertaken thus far, and timelines for completing the remainder of planned activities. The discussion should include gains in knowledge, skill, disposition, and effects on learning and district improvement. The formative evaluations should note any changes to the plan. Changes should have a brief explanation of the circumstances and rationale for the change.

3.8   Final Professional Report Development

Interns should review the requirements for the Professional Portfolio or Report in the next Stage. Please note that preparations programs might use other summative evaluations or add additional requirements. Be sure to check with your program advisor to determine exactly which requirements are in place. If some form of a summative portfolio or report is used, it is highly recommended that the intern work on the portfolio or report as they move forward in the internship versus waiting until the end. The portfolio or report must be organized for professional presentation, similar to reporting to the Board. Documentation should include:

- ◆ Activities completed from the NELP standard activities.
- ◆ Service activities.
- ◆ Independent leading activities.
- ◆ Performance assessment tasks, project, or reports, or inquiry-based project or action research study.
- ◆ Other required documentation, i.e., log, reflections, etc.

References

Baumann, L., & Utz, S. (2021). Professional networking: Exploring differences between offline and online networking. *Cyberpsychology: Journal of Psychosocial Research on Cyberspace*, 15(1), Article 2. https://doi.org/10.5817/CP2021-1-2

Bernhardt, V. (2006). *Using data to improve student learning in school districts*. Larchmont, NY: Eye on Education.

Bernhardt, V. L. (2015). *Data, data everywhere: bringing all the data together for continuous school improvement*. C/O Kentucky District Center, 7625 Empire Dr, Florence, KY: Taylor & Francis.

Bryk, A. S., Gomez, L., Grunow, A., & LeMahieu, P. (2015). *Learning to improve. How America's schools can get better at getting better*. Cambridge, MA: Harvard Education Press.

Darling-Hammond, L., LaPointe, M., Meyerson, D., Orr. M. T., & Cohen, C. (2007). *Preparing school leaders for a changing world: Lessons from exemplary leadership development programs*. Stanford, CA: Stanford University, Stanford Educational Leadership Institute. https://edpolicy.stanford.edu/sites/default/files/publications/preparing-school-leaders-changing-world-lessons-exemplary-leadership-development-programs_1.pdf

Dickmann, M. H., & Stanford-Blair, N. (2002). *Connecting leadership to the brain*. Thousand Oaks, CA: Corwin Press.

Fergus, E. (2016). *Solving disproportionality and achieving equity: a leader's guide to using data to change hearts and minds*. Thousand Oaks, CA: Corwin Press C/O Sage Publications.

Forman, M. L., Stosich, E. L., & Bocala, C. (2017). *The Internal Coherence Framework: Creating the Conditions for Continuous Improvement in Schools*. Cambridge, MA: Harvard Education Press.

Gannon-Slater, N., La Londe, P., Crenshaw, H., Evans, M., Greene, J. & Schwandt, T. (2017). Advancing equity in accountability and organizational cultures of data use. *Journal of Educational Administration*, 55 (4), 361–375. https://doi.org/10.1108/JEA-09-2016-0168

Kolb, D. A., Boyatzis, R. E., & Charalampos, M. (2001). *Experiential learning theory: Previous research and new directions*. New York: Routledge.

Lasater, K., Albiladi, W., Davis, W., & Bengston, E. (2020). The data culture continuum: An examination of school data cultures. *Educational Administration Quarterly*, 56(4), 533–569. https://doi.org/10.1177/0013161X19873034

LinkedIn, (2019). About Linkedin [Statistics Page]. Retrieved from: https://news.linkedin.com/about-us#statistics

Militello, M., Rallis, S. F., & Goldring, E. B. (2009). *Leading with inquiry & action*. Thousand Oaks, CA: Corwin Press.

Porter, C. M., & Woo, S. E. (2015). Untangling the networking phenomenon: A dynamic psychological perspective on how and why people network. *Journal of Management*, 41(5), 1477–1500. https//doi.org/10.1177/0149206315582247

Schildkamp, K., Poortman, C. L., Ebbeler, J., & Pieters, J. M. (2019). How school leaders can build effective data teams: Five building blocks for a new wave of data-informed decision making. *Journal of Educational Change*, 20(3), 283. https//doi.org/10.1007/s10833-019-09345-3

Spurk, D., Hirschi, A., & Dries, N. (2019). Antecedents and outcomes of objective versus subjective career success: Competing perspectives and future directions. *Journal of Management*, 45(2019), 35–69. https//doi.org/10.1177/0149206318786563

Totoro, G. (2017). What's your networking IQ? Eight steps to improve your score. Retrieved from: www.forbes.com/sites/forbescoachescouncil/2017/04/14/whats-your-networking-iq-eight-steps-to-improve-your-score/#20cf25b11e56

Internship Summative Assessment/Final Report

In this final stage, the intern will prepare and present the concluding summative report. University or preparation program requirements may vary so be certain to check with your program advisor. Typically, the intern will present the report and/or portfolio to their program advisor. The report should be a professional presentation, similar to reporting to the Board. Documentation should include the items listed below. We strongly recommend that you share your final report and/or portfolio with your district internship supervisor for feedback on your growth and development. It can also be a useful resource for your supervisor in preparing your letter of recommendation when seeking your initial district leader position.

4.1 Internship Log

The completed log must be submitted in accordance with your program requirements. The log should include but is not limited to the following:

- Beginning and ending dates of the internship.
- Total number of hours and approximate percentages of hours observing, participating, and leading.
- Brief description of activities and dates performed.
- Name and title of district supervisor and contact information.
- Other program requirements.

4.2 NELP Professional Standards Assessment

The intern must complete a summary and evaluation of experience for each of the seven NELP professional standards and/or other standards used by the program. One summary and evaluation for each area is required, regardless of the amount of time or number of activities accomplished in the leadership standard. The summary and evaluation of each standard should be approximately one page and include the following:

- Overview/summary of activities performed for the standard.
- Key learnings from the experience (knowledge, skill, and/or disposition).
- Area(s) needing further experience and improvement.
- Personal assessment of the degree of mastery of the standard.

DOI: 10.4324/9781003299493-5

This assessment enables you to reflect upon your growth and development in each set of standards-defined skills and show the breadth and depth of your exposure, experiences, and accomplishments. Using this assessment, evaluate your growth and development: How and in what ways have you been prepared for district leadership? In what areas have you experienced leadership growth and development the most? Where further development is critical?

4.3   Dispositions Assessment

The intern should retake the Disposition Assessment found in Stage 1 as a post-assessment and compare results with the initial or pre-assessment. Briefly describe the dispositions that were focused upon during the internship and provide evidence (new beliefs, feelings, actions taken, etc.) that show a positive change in the disposition. Also, highlight dispositions that need further development and how these will be addressed in the future.

4.4   Reflective Practice Assessment

Competence grows as one observes more. The goal was to observe more and have a greater range of models to draw from as you reflected on your own actions and the actions of others. The intern will summarize and provide highlights of their experience with reflective practice. Briefly discuss the following:

+ What models/concepts/theories were effective or not effective?
+ What deep-seated beliefs guided your actions and experience?
+ How did the history/traditions/culture of the district affect your actions?
+ How did your emotional state/moods affect your actions and experience?
+ How did the availability or lack of resources affect your actions?
+ How did the on-the-job experience change your beliefs and actions?
+ How and in what ways have you been prepared for district leadership? In what areas have you experienced leadership growth and development the most? Where is further development critical?
+ How have your instructional leadership skills improved since you began the program? What internship experiences contributed to this development and improvement?
+ How has your understanding of the role of leadership to foster social justice and promote equity changed throughout the program? How has your internship contributed to your understanding? What leadership skills have you developed to support this role?
+ In what ways did you contribute to district improvement through your internship? What leadership skills and practices did you use? What challenges did you experience and what have you learned for your future work as a district leader?
+ How has your commitment to a career in district leadership changed through the internship and what are your current goals?

4.5   Foundational Leadership Skills Development

The intern will include a brief (1/2 to 1 page each) description of two or more of the 12 foundational skills that were focused on during the internship. Cite examples of activities or experiences that were undertaken and briefly describe the learning from the activity or experience. Cite two additional foundational skills that you plan to focus on in the future.

4.6   Independent Leadership Assessment

Throughout the internship, interns will be asked to complete large assignments or work products or conduct an inquiry-based project such as action research project or district improvement planning project. These may be the large assignments detailed in this handbook or assignments outlined by leadership preparation program expectations (such as performance assessment tasks) or district internship supervisor. Interns should compile a written summary of completed work and include the following:

- Description of the project.
- Goals of the project.
- Results/findings from the project.
- Implications and next steps.
- Intern's role and responsibilities.
- Reflection on lessons learned on leading the project.

4.7   Impact on Student Learning and/ or Learning Environment

The role of an educational leader is to increase student learning outcomes and provide an effective and supporting learning environment. Review the logs and reflective journal and cite examples of actions taken that demonstrate a positive impact on increased student learning and/or an improved learning environment. If performance assessment tasks, work products or action research project were conducted, these should be included in this section with a clear explanation of their alignment to improving student learning and/or environment. The intent of this section is to demonstrate the ability to recognize the relationship between leadership action and student performance.

4.8   District Improvement Recommendations

Interns have unique perspectives on district leadership. From your perspective, develop a prioritized list of recommendations for overall district improvement. The list may include recommendations for leaders, teachers, staff, parents, and/or community members. The list may also include recommendations for curriculum, instructions, assessment, discipline, or any other areas you believe can be improved and lead to greater student learning and satisfaction with the school experience.

4.9   Updated Resume/Vita

The intern should update their resume/vita to include relevant accomplishments from the internship. This may be included in the leadership section of the vita for those not currently holding an administrative or supervisory position. Guidelines for developing the resume/vita are listed in Appendix A.1. A copy of the updated resume/vita should be included in the final internship report.

4.10   Letter of Interest

The letter of application should focus on the specific career goal of the intern. For example, if the intern wants the position of district curriculum director, the letter of interest should be written for that position. If the intern would want an assistant superintendent position prior to applying for a superintendency, the letter should be written for that position. Guidelines for the letter of application are listed in Appendix A.2. The letter of application should be included in the final internship report.

4.11   Future Professional Development Plan

The intern must prepare and submit a three-year professional development plan based on their internship experience. Typically, a professional development plan focuses on the priorities or greatest needs of the leader. The plan must be clear, manageable, and include a means of evaluation.

A clear plan lists specific objectives. These may include skill development, reevaluating dispositions, attaining new knowledge, etc. It should cite actions to be taken, as opposed to a vague or general intent to improve in a particular area. This could include additional courses, workshops, books, working with a mentor, or a host of other experiences. The intern should research available resources to meet their objectives. Exact titles or dates of future training may not be available at this time.

A plan that is manageable includes actions that can be accomplished in a reasonable amount of time. Typically, three to five objectives are included in a three-year plan. This allows the intern time to use or practice the new knowledge, disposition, or skill. A timeline for each objective must be included. The plan must cite the criteria used to judge whether the objective was met. Ideally, this would be an artifact or other evidence.

4.12   Developing a Portfolio

A portfolio is a compilation of relevant evidence of your knowledge, skill, and disposition. It may include degrees and certificates but is primarily the best sample of your professional work and accomplishments. It is recommended that you use the NELP standards as your portfolio sections and provide evidence that you meet or are progressing in meeting these standards.

At this point in your leadership development, it is understood that you may not have documentation or evidence of meeting all the standards. This is the beginning of your portfolio, however, and should serve to guide the planning of future professional development. Submit the portfolio or link to the e-portfolio, if applicable. Check with the university or program advisor for specific requirements for a portfolio or other means for documentation storage or presentation.

Appendices

 **Appendix A.1**

Sample Resume/Vita and Guidelines

George E. Washington

500 Pennsylvania Avenue

Globe, Arizona 75000

(W) (808) 555-4202; (H) (808) 555-7171; gwashington@hotmail.com

---

Education/Certification

M.Ed.	Educational Leadership, Northern Arizona University, Flagstaff, AZ., 2019
B.A.	English, Carleton College, Northfield, MN, 2010
Superintendent Certificate	Arizona
Principal Certificate	Arizona
Teacher Certificate	Language Arts (6-12), Arizona and Minnesota
	Mathematics (1-8), Arizona and Minnesota
	Self-Contained (1-8), Arizona and Minnesota
ESL Endorsement	(PK-12), Arizona and Minnesota

Leadership Experience

Curriculum and Instruction Director, Mt. Vernon School District, Vernon, AZ, 2018–present.

- Directed, evaluated, and provided leadership for the overall instructional program
- Oversaw compliance with district policies, supervision of campus personnel, educational welfare of students, and safekeeping of school property
- Led, taught, and trained professional colleagues to disaggregate data and implement data-driven decisions
- Provided Trainer-of-Trainer program for department and grade level chairs
- Supervised districtwide curriculum mapping project

District Program Support Specialist, Mt. Vernon School District, Vernon, AZ, 2017–2018.

- Planned, implemented, monitored, and evaluated the implementation of Section 504, RtI, and dyslexia programs to support and enhance student achievement
- Monitored and evaluated procedures for district-wide implementation and consistency regarding Section 504, Response to Intervention (RtI), and dyslexia
- Conducted dyslexia assessments, compile testing data, and review testing results with appropriate campus personnel and parents
- Served as district 504 Coordinator and ensured district compliance
- Served as a district resource person regarding dyslexia, Section 504, and RtI
- Worked closely with Special Education Department and diagnosticians for RtI Reviews
- Advised Superintendent on Special Program Issues

Copyright material from Gary E. Martin, Jimmy R. Creel, Thomas W. Harvey, Robert E. Nicks, and Michael Schwanenberger (2023), *District Leader Internship*, Routledge

Principal, Appomattox High School, Kingman, AZ 2012–2017
- Supervised high school campus of 2,500 students and 175 staff & faculty
- Led campus to top state academic ratings for four out of five years
- Created and taught Appomattox Future Administrators seminars — helped prepare 23 faculty members who were selected for administrative positions
- Chaired numerous committees for school improvement issues

Assistant Principal, Sand Dune Elementary, Kingman, AZ 2010–2012
- Served as campus 504 and Rtl coordinator and summer school principal
- Served as campus behavior coordinator
- Supervised, coached, and evaluated teachers
- Led the update of the Campus Improvement Plan
- Assisted in coordinating transportation, custodial, cafeteria, and other school support services; help conduct safety inspections and safety drill practice activities
- Created master schedule

Teaching Experience

English Department Chairperson, Martha High School, Mt. Vernon, AZ 2007–2010.
- Designed a department-based professional literacy library and conference center to help teachers better their pedagogical skills.
- Implemented an English department collaborative teaching plan that promoted positive teacher communication regarding units and lessons, methodology, classroom management, and student achievement.
- Planned and presented various English department in-services designed to improve classroom instruction, time management, and grant writing.
- Evaluated all English teachers using the district's evaluation instrument and informal observations while carefully monitoring the progress of new and inexperienced teachers.

High School English Teacher, Martha High School, Mt. Vernon, AZ, 2003–2007.
- Integrated a variety of teaching methods and instructional strategies to generate student interest.
- Evaluated and tracked student progress in class by using a combination of evaluations and student work samples.
- Maintained positive relationship with students and parents while holding students to a high standard of acceptable class work.

Copyright material from Gary E. Martin, Jimmy R. Creel, Thomas W. Harvey, Robert E. Nicks, and Michael Schwanenberger (2023), *District Leader Internship*, Routledge

Designed a writing workshop for students involved to create, edit, and revise their own work in a summer writing portfolio.

Published a variety of works from every student's summer writing portfolio in a book distributed to all students and parents at the end of the summer.

Coaching Experience

Head Basketball Coach, Martha High School, Mt. Vernon, AZ, 2004–2007.

Incorporated a successful parent booster club that raised funds to support the basketball program.

Created a successful basketball program that won at least 19 games in each of the last three seasons while maintaining a team grade point average greater than 3.2.

Additional Training/Professional Development

"Cutting Edge Grant Writing", Otter Creek Institute, Phoenix, AZ, May 2010.

"Increasing Student Achievement", National School Conference Institute, Phoenix, AZ, March 2012.

Presentations

Washington, G. (2009, September). *Improving Student Writing*. Presentation at the Inter-District Articulation Program, Mt. Vernon, AZ.

Washington, G. (2008, September). *Incorporating Writing in all Classrooms*. Presentation at the Martha High School Faculty In-service, Mt. Vernon, AZ.

Washington, G. (2007, August). *NCA Writing Goal and the Six-Trait Writing Rubric*. Presentation at the Martha High School In-service Program, Mt. Vernon, AZ.

Professional Affiliations

Association for Supervision and Curriculum Development, 2006–present

National Association of Secondary School Principals, 2012–present

Arizona Professional Educators, 2012–present

References

References will be supplied upon request.

Copyright material from Gary E. Martin, Jimmy R. Creel, Thomas W. Harvey, Robert E. Nicks, and Michael Schwanenberger (2023), *District Leader Internship*, Routledge

Guidelines for the Development of the Resume/Vita

Webster's On-Line Dictionary (2018) as well as the Collins On-Line Dictionary (2018) describes the word "vita" as a noun and the word "vitae" as the plural form of the noun. Both dictionaries define the word vita as 1) A biography or autobiography, often a short one; 2) Curriculum vitae. A curriculum vitae (CV) can be defined as an outline of a person's educational and professional history and typically prepared for job applications. In the public education arena, the terms vita, vitae, curriculum vitae, and resume are often used interchangeably. For our purposes, all terms refer to a thorough, but succinct outline of one's educational background, credentials, and professional history.

Since the superintendent position is unique among school employment positions, we believe that the vita prepared to solicit consideration as a superintendent is also somewhat unique among such documents. Why do we suggest that the superintendent position is unique among school employees? Here are a few of the reasons:

- There is only one superintendent in each district.
- There is only one employee in most districts who is employed under a negotiated contract.
- There is only one employee in most districts who reports directly and exclusively to the board of trustees – unless your district employs an internal auditor. In that case, there may be two employees in the district who report directly to the board of trustees.
- There is only one employee in the district who is ultimately responsible for the budget, for oversight of all revenue, for supervision of all employees, and for legal compliance with laws and regulations.

These are just a few of the reasons that we believe the superintendent position is unique among all school district positions. As such, we believe that the superintendent vita should be tailored to fit the job responsibilities and expectations of the position. The customization of the vita to address the varied responsibilities of the position is likely to require a vita that is also somewhat unique. In other words, the superintendent vita may legitimately include some information that would not be relevant or critical for other positions within the district. For example, an elementary principal need not document his/her expertise in creating, training, and maintaining a "Team of 8" relationship with the board of trustees. The superintendent vita certainly should validate the candidate's capacity to be successful in such an endeavor. Because of the "uniqueness" of the superintendent responsibilities and the variation of required skills and knowledge, the vita prepared for an aspiring superintendent may be somewhat longer than a typical vita or resume.

There are generally three documents that will be critical to your quest to become a superintendent. Those documents include the district application, the letter of interest, and the vita. The district application is obviously specific to an individual district and the letter of interest should also be tailored specifically to the needs of each specific district in which you might make application for consideration as the superintendent of schools. Both documents are critical to your success in being considered for the top position in any school district. However, since they are somewhat specific, they generally cannot be developed until a position becomes open and the applicant is aware of the specific requirements of a district. We do not believe that it is best practice to create a "generic" letter of interest that one sends

Copyright material from Gary E. Martin, Jimmy R. Creel, Thomas W. Harvey, Robert E. Nicks, and Michael Schwanenberger (2023), *District Leader Internship*, Routledge

to all districts. Conversely, the vita can and should be developed prior to an opening developing. For that reason, we encourage you to develop your vita now and to be sure that the vita is kept up to date. One never knows when an opening will occur and your vita needs to be complete, up-to-date, and ready to submit quickly when an opening that interests you does develop.

The completion of the application and the development of a letter of interest will keep you busy as you prepare to submit application materials. Other application materials that a district may request as part of the application process include original transcripts, handwritten philosophy of education or a handwritten memo to address a hypothetical situation, letters of recommendation, and documentation of certifications and required training for conducting evaluations, safety and security, and other administrative specialty areas. Some of these documents can be obtained and prepared for future job applications. However, not all districts require such documents, and it may not be efficient use of your time to seek all these documents and prepare them before they are needed. The vita, however, will be required in every district or, at least, the information on the vita will be required in every district as part of the application process. Let's think about ways that you can begin now to create, update, and maintain a vita that is ready to use.

Your vita has one main purpose. That purpose is to help the search consultant or the board of trustees see you as an applicant with potential to add value to the district in the top leadership position and an applicant whom the consultant feels the board should interview, or if the board is reviewing application materials, that the board determines they should interview for the purpose of further exploring whether or not the skills, credentials, and experience you offer matches the perception of the board regarding the needs of the district. Your goal when you submit the application materials should be to secure an interview with the board. That is the first hurdle that must be passed.

Consequently, you should pay careful attention to every document that is submitted as part of your application packet. To prepare a vita that convinces the search consultant or board members that you would be worth the time and energy required to further explore your potential as the district's next superintendent, you should consider the following items as you develop your vita. There is no set formula or template for preparing a superintendent vita.

A vita is a concise, often bulleted, summary of your education and training, experience, accomplishments, expertise, and work history. To prepare for the development and updating of your vita, there are a few steps you can take.

Accomplishments

List all your accomplishments. Use action verbs to describe the accomplishments and goals you have achieved. After listing all the accomplishments of which you are aware, evaluate the list and attempt to prioritize. Choose the top five accomplishments. Then, go through the remaining items two or three at a time and ask yourself if those items are more important than the five you have already chosen. If so, replace items in the original top five. If you identify items that are just as important as the top five you have identified, add them to the list. There is no set number or requirement (Corda, 2012).

Work History

Use your service record or other resources to list chronologically all your adult work history. Be sure there are NO GAPS in the list.

Copyright material from Gary E. Martin, Jimmy R. Creel, Thomas W. Harvey, Robert E. Nicks, and Michael Schwanenberger (2023), *District Leader Internship*, Routledge

Explanations

Perhaps, you started your career in education and worked for eight years and then sold insurance for the next five years and returned to education after that. Rather than leave a five-year gap in your work history, be sure that there is a clear explanation in the vita for your absence from education-related employment. There is nothing wrong with going into business to earn more money to support your family. You just need to make sure it is clearly indicated in your vita. Under no circumstances should you leave an unexplained gap of time in your work history. Employers will interpret such a gap as an attempt to hide some unstated adversarial employment history in most cases.

Other explanations may be needed for issues that are not so blatant (Corda, 2012). For example, suppose that you got out of coaching in 2000 to move into an assistant principal position. Suppose that the principal left in 2002 and you applied for the job and were appointed as the principal. Suppose that a principal position in a neighboring district came open in 2004 which was considered a professional advancement, and which paid an additional $15,000. You were selected for the job. In 2005, a central office administrator in your new district died and the superintendent asked you to fill the position in October of that year. Suppose in 2006, you accepted a central office position in your original district that was also considered a professional advancement and included a $10,000 raise. If you allow your vita to reflect four professional moves in six years without an appropriate explanation for the moves, a board may interpret that many moves in that period as a sign that you were not meeting expectations in your work and that you would not be a quality candidate for their position. Do not allow the potential for such a misinterpretation of the facts. Be sure that the board has a full understanding of the rationale and reasoning behind such professional mobility. Also, if there are personal issues that could concern the board or precipitate questions, be sure to explain. A pending divorce or a foreclosure on your record should be disclosed and explained. Do not let some seemingly unrelated issue or incident cause you to be excluded from consideration.

References

Pay attention to the selection of references. Choose references who can and will validate the information you provide on your vita. Be sure that the contact information you provide for each reference is accurate and effective in contacting the reference. In many cases, boards have so many good candidates for a superintendent position that any difficulty in contacting a reference can be a reason for your exclusion from consideration. Do your best to minimize the possibility that the board or its designee will have any difficulty in communicating with your reference. BE AWARE! Good consultants who have been in the superintendent search business for a while will often try to identify individuals in your district whom you have NOT listed as a reference to call to seek information on your work, your ethics, and your leadership skills. If you have other network contacts outside the district such as the region service center or other points of contact, those individuals are often targets for additional research as well. In other words, do your best not to create too many enemies inside or outside the district. One never knows with whom the board will eventually communicate (Corda, 2012).

Things to Not Include

As stated previously, the resume/vita for a superintendent position may be longer than a vita for other educational positions. However, you should do your best to ensure that the vita is as succinct as possible. One way to do this is to review the information on the vita

Copyright material from Gary E. Martin, Jimmy R. Creel, Thomas W. Harvey, Robert E. Nicks, and Michael Schwanenberger (2023), *District Leader Internship*, Routledge

carefully to ensure that it is needed to communicate your strength as a candidate for the position. Your goal should be to list experience that is both timely and relevant (Burry, 2018).

Jargon and Acronyms

Watch for excessive jargon and acronyms in your vita. While some board members are savvy to such nomenclature, many are not. Remember, most board members are not educators. Try to communicate without excessive jargon and spell out acronyms so that there is no miscommunication (Burry, 2018).

Edit, Re-edit, and Have Others Edit

Our final advice is to proofread, proofread, and proofread your vita again and again. Look for content errors, spelling errors, punctuation errors, grammar errors, and any other kind of mistake. Your goal should be to ELIMINATE all errors. Remember, this document, along with the other application materials, is the only representation of you that the board will see until they invite you for an interview. Not only should YOU read and re-read the document searching for errors, but you should also ask a close friend or associate or your spouse to do the same. It often takes an "outside set of eyes" to spot mistakes. Those who review vitae and résumés regularly often assume that a document with errors is a representation of a candidate that does not have the work ethic to lead their district. Do not let this happen to you. Eliminate errors.

Keep Your Resume/Vita Updated

It is easier to keep your vita updated as you go than to wait several years and attempt to update. As experiences occur or training takes place or honors are awarded, decide then if the item merits addition to your vita. At the same time, consider discarding older components of your vita. Keep the vita updated and ready to go. You never know when you will need it quickly.

Overall Guidelines
1) Well defined categories/sections in appropriate order
2) Neat and conservative (on white or beige, more space than type)
3) Accurate and ethical
4) Accomplishment oriented
5) Results of accomplishments shown, if any (supportive evidence in portfolio)
6) Information outside of professional life omitted
7) Clear, readable font (size 12 for most fonts)
8) Grammatically correct (consistent use of past tense verbs)
9) Several pages in length (not the one-page business resume)

Preferred Order of Categories

Choose the categories that are most accurate, ethical, and appropriate. Other categories or combinations of these and others for unique individuals and/or experiences may be used.

Heading
Education/Certification,
Administrative, Supervisory, and/or Leadership Experience,
Teaching Experience,

Copyright material from Gary E. Martin, Jimmy R. Creel, Thomas W. Harvey, Robert E. Nicks, and Michael Schwanenberger (2023), *District Leader Internship*, Routledge

Coaching Experience (if applicable),
Related Experience (if applicable),
Other Experience (if applicable),
Professional Development,
Publications and/or Presentations and/or Grants (if applicable),
Curriculum Experience (if applicable),
Professional Affiliations,
Honors and/or Awards (if applicable),
Community Involvement/Service,
Professional References,
Reference page.

Heading Guidelines

a) Heading should be 3 lines in length.
b) Name should stand out and be legal name.
c) Provide complete address, phone number(s) with area codes, and e-mail.

Education/Certification Category Guidelines

a) Degree should be highlighted.
b) Following degree is area of degree, institution, city, state, and year awarded.
c) Major and/or minor may be listed, if appropriate and useful.
d) Address of institution is not needed.
e) Note any significant number of hours taken, not leading to degree.
f) Skip one line to separate certificates from degrees.
g) Certificates are cited exactly as written on certificate and include State.
h) List administrative certificate(s) first.
i) Place any endorsements after teaching certificates.
j) Include current certification sought – use (In Progress) or (Expected completion date, [month and year]).

Administrative and/or Leadership Category Guidelines

a) Use Administrative Experience category only if you were certified and served in an administrative position. It is unethical to invent a title, i.e., Assistant Principal, if you only assisted the principal.
b) Use Supervisory Experience category only if you were certified and served in a supervisory position (supervising adults).
c) Use Leadership Experience category for all other leadership roles, i.e., Department or Grade Level Chair, Committee Chair, Site Council Member, etc.
d) Categories are combinable, for example, Supervisory/Leadership Experience, if experience in both.
e) List title first, then school, city, state, and date(s).
f) Use bullets and relevant past tense verbs for all accomplishments, for example, wrote, implemented, supervised, etc.
g) List any results of accomplishment, if known and appropriate.
h) Use two to six bullets under each title.

Copyright material from Gary E. Martin, Jimmy R. Creel, Thomas W. Harvey, Robert E. Nicks, and Michael Schwanenberger (2023), *District Leader Internship*, Routledge

Teaching Experience Category Guidelines

a) Capitalize and list title first, then organization or school, city, state, and date(s).

b) Use bullets and relevant past tense verbs, for example, wrote, implemented, supervised, etc.

c) List any results of accomplishment, if known.

d) Use two to six bullets, typically more if very recent or significant number of years in the following format:

Title, organization or school, city, state, date(s)

* Past tense verb + accomplishment + results
* Past tense verb + accomplishment + results
* Past tense verb + accomplishment
* Past tense verb + accomplishment

Coaching, Related, and/or Other Experience Category Guidelines

a) Use the same format as above under Teaching Experience guidelines.

b) Use Coaching Experience category if duty was contracted and experience was significant. List minor coaching duties as bullet(s) under Teaching Experience category.

c) Use Related Experience category if duties are related to teaching/administrative duties.

d) Use Other Experience category if significant experience, i.e., former career, etc.

Professional Development Category Guidelines

a) Cite the title first, then organization, city, state, and date(s).

b) There is no limit to the number of citations in this category.

c) All training cited should be relevant to education/leadership.

d) Note number of hours (if a significant amount).

Presentations and/or Publications Category Guidelines

a) Cite all presentations and/or publications in APA or other appropriate formats.

b) For five or fewer citations, use combination of categories – Presentations/ Publications. If more than five and at least two in each, use separate Presentation and Publication categories.

c) Be sure to include all co-authors or co-presenters.

d) Consider citing dissertations, theses, and locally published curricular materials.

Professional Affiliations Category Guidelines

a) Cite all current memberships in professional organizations.

b) Note any offices held.

c) Cite membership in any professional organizations of significant duration.

d) Spell out complete names of organizations – do not use acronyms.

Honors/Awards/Scholarship Category Guidelines

a) Use relevant category if you have two or more citations – otherwise, list under Teaching or Administrative category.

Copyright material from Gary E. Martin, Jimmy R. Creel, Thomas W. Harvey, Robert E. Nicks, and Michael Schwanenberger (2023), *District Leader Internship*, Routledge

b) Use combination of categories, if appropriate.

c) Cite Honor, Award, or Scholarship, then organization, city/state, and date.

Civic/Community Service Category Guidelines

a) List title, organization, city, state, and date(s).

b) Service should be related to goals or duties of the education profession instead of purely personal.

c) Service to a particular church or religion may be used or if viewed as personal information, should not be cited.

References Category Guidelines

a) Use as last category on vita.

b) It is unethical to include references with vita, unless references requested.

c) Be sure references gave permission to use their names.

References Page Guidelines

a) List name and title first.

b) List name of school or organization next.

c) List complete address, city, state, and zip code.

d) List phone number with area code and email address.

e) This must be a separate page.

f) Cite no more than 6 references.

g) Must have reference for each place worked – if more than six, stay within last 10 years.

h) Try to use administrator references – personal references are not appropriate.

i) Cite references in order of priority – often only the first three are contacted.

j) Ensure that all individuals listed as references are willing and able to comment on your performance, skill, and knowledge based on their personal experience and observation.

k) Ensure that all contact information for references is current, up-to-date, and viable.

Sample reference page listing:

Dr. Bill Hickok, Principal
Page Elementary
184 Avenue C
Tombstone, AZ 85365
(520) 783-9999; bh@isp.edu

Frequently Asked Questions

Q: Shouldn't the vita be organized by years and have them in the left margin?

A: No. That is a style used for a business resume, not an educational vita. However, a chronological timeline for professional experience should be easily discernible. Search consultants and boards are interested in following a candidate's professional experience and ensuring that any gaps in experience are explained or accounted for.

Copyright material from Gary E. Martin, Jimmy R. Creel, Thomas W. Harvey, Robert E. Nicks, and Michael Schwanenberger (2023), *District Leader Internship*, Routledge

Q: Should I use expensive paper with bright colors to make it stand out?

A: Neither expensive nor inexpensive paper is necessary, but you may use a good-quality paper. Brightly colored paper is a tactic used in the world of business. Your experience and accomplishments should stand out, not the color of the paper.

Q: What if I have gaps of time in my vita?

A: You should exercise good judgment in this case. Often those with gaps in their career are raising children or tending to a sick family member or any other reasonable use of their time. There are others, however, that were fired and could not get another job, were in drug rehabilitation, or any other very personal reason. The point is that the reviewer of your vita may have doubts about which group you are in. Thus, unless your reasons are extremely personal, it is recommended that you provide some explanation for gaps in time to prevent the doubts of prospective employers.

Q: I do not have much in the leadership category. Should I list "leading students" in various activities or groups?

A: Your inexperience with leadership should motivate you to volunteer or apply for positions that will give you the necessary experience. Do not wait for an administrative position to gain leadership experience. There are many committees to chair, councils to serve on, and programs to lead while still teaching. Use your vita as a learning experience and start filling in the gaps.

Q: What if my coaching experience is quite extensive?

A: This is another judgment call. Much will depend on the position you are applying for. If, for example, you are applying for an Athletic Director position, then a complete listing of your coaching experience would be appropriate. If you were applying for solely an Assistant Principal position, then you would limit your coaching experience category and use as much as appropriate in the leadership experience category. Many duties and responsibilities in athletics leadership are the same as in school administration.

Q: What if I do not belong to any professional organizations?

A: It's time to join! Choose what is appropriate to your career goals. High school and middle level principals may join the National Association of Secondary School Administrators (NASSP), elementary principals may join the National Association of Elementary Principals (NAESP), and those interested in curriculum development may join the Association for Supervision and Curriculum Development (ASCD). It is recommended that you also become active in the state affiliations for these professional organizations and read their journals regularly. Again, you do not have to wait to get the position to learn more about the position.

Q: What if I do not have any awards or honors?

A: Many great educators never received any honors or awards. Others were honored or recognized after their career ended. Honors and awards are bestowed on you by others – do not seek awards or honors, but graciously accept them.

Q: Should I or shouldn't I list church activities?

A: In public education, we are bound by separation of church and state. While active involvement with a particular church may denote many positive aspects of your service and character, it may also be viewed by some as interfering with the goals of public education. This is another judgment you must make.

With your vita, letter of application, and interview, your responsibility is to clearly show the prospective school district who you are. This is your half of the work leading

Copyright material from Gary E. Martin, Jimmy R. Creel, Thomas W. Harvey, Robert E. Nicks, and Michael Schwanenberger (2023), *District Leader Internship*, Routledge

up to the contract. If a religious affiliation is such a big part of you that it goes with you into school, then it would be appropriate to cite your church work. If your religious affiliation is more personal in nature and is not brought into the school, then omitting it from your professional vita would be appropriate.

Q: Why must the reference page be separate?

A: Persons willing to provide reference information for you are assuming districts very interested in hiring you will contact them. They should not have to provide information to every district where you applied. Therefore, it is considered unethical to provide references, unless requested in the job announcement or by the employer.

Q: Why list accomplishments?

A: Leaders accomplish things! This includes all educational leaders, especially teachers. A vita that shows only where and when you worked does not give any indication of accomplishment. Did you simply show up every day, or did you set goals and accomplish them? Accomplishment-oriented vitae do a much better job of showing who the leaders are. You should spend time analyzing your accomplishments (often forgotten or taken for granted) and list under the appropriate position.

Q: Is the vita changeable?

A: Although one cannot change the facts, one can add facts and/or present them differently. Design the vita according to the position sought. For example, the district may desire curricular experience for the position. In this case, an applicant could include a Curriculum Experience category and place it higher up in the list of categories used.

Copyright material from Gary E. Martin, Jimmy R. Creel, Thomas W. Harvey, Robert E. Nicks, and Michael Schwanenberger (2023), *District Leader Internship*, Routledge

Appendix A.2

Sample Letter of Interest and Guidelines

Ms. Joan Jackson, President
Educational Consultants USA, LLC
14000 Cedar Blvd., Suite 5000
Meyers, CO 61644

Dear Ms. Jackson,

I have read the position announcement for the XYZ Independent School District Superintendent of Schools and wish to be considered for the position. Upon review of the requested personal characteristics, experience, certification, and professional attributes for the new superintendent, I meet or exceed all the requirements listed in the position announcement and I look forward to your review of my qualifications.

It is my belief that the district superintendent should have extensive administrative experience at the school level and have a thorough understanding of the teaching and learning process. This belief aligns with the XYZ Board of Trustees as they have identified school-based administrative experience and a thorough knowledge of pedagogy as prerequisites for the superintendent position. I have had the pleasure to successfully lead an elementary campus for six years and a high school campus for four years. Both campuses received high district and state ratings associated with student academic performance. In both principal experiences, student performance improved each year. Utilizing a democratic leadership style, empowering teachers and staff with appropriate resources and professional development, and establishing high expectations were key elements to achieving success. In other words, it was a team effort. This will be the same philosophical approach that will be used in my next assignment as a superintendent of schools.

Leading a small to mid-size school district involves a commitment from not only the applicant, but the applicant's family as well. Please know that my family and I have discussed the possibility of a move to XYZ, and we are thrilled with the prospect. My wife and I and our two school-age children have always been involved with school activities, our local church, and community organizations and will continue to do so in XYZ if fortunate enough to be selected for this position. Based on ten years' administrative experience in the same school district, the Board of Trustees may feel confident that I am grounded and value the stability of my family and school district.

The opportunity to work in concert with a dedicated Board of Trustees is a significant factor in my decision to seek the superintendent's position. During my superintendent internship and with the mentorship of an excellent superintendent, I have viewed first-hand the importance of effective communications, operational transparency, and the importance of recognizing and respecting the role of board trustee and the role of the superintendent. Controversial issues will be decided only after adequate input is received from those affected and tough decisions will be defended with adequate rationale and clearly communicated.

Copyright material from Gary E. Martin, Jimmy R. Creel, Thomas W. Harvey, Robert E. Nicks, and Michael Schwanenberger (2023), *District Leader Internship*, Routledge

Thank you for reviewing my application and I hope to have the opportunity to interview with the Board of Trustees. If additional information is needed or if you have questions pertaining to my application, please do not hesitate to contact me.

Respectfully yours,

Edwin R. Jones, Principal
ABC High School

Copyright material from Gary E. Martin, Jimmy R. Creel, Thomas W. Harvey, Robert E. Nicks, and Michael Schwanenberger (2023), *District Leader Internship*, Routledge

Review the Position Announcement

Applications for a school district superintendent position should always be specific to the individual district and developed based upon information contained in the position announcement. Language in the position announcement should be reflected in your application materials, e.g., if the position announcement references a vita, provide a vita as opposed to a resume, if the position announcement indicates that the applicant should provide proof of state superintendent certification, be sure to include a copy of your certificate with your application materials, etc. Utilize the position announcement as a guide for both documentation and content of your application materials.

Sample Position Announcement

The XYZ Independent School District Board of Trustees is seeking an educational leader to serve as the Superintendent of Schools. The successful candidate must possess the following characteristics and qualifications:

- Possess State Superintendent Certification.
- A willingness to reside in the school district.
- A proven leader who has served as an educator with at least 5 years administrative experience.
- An effective communicator who is willing to defend and make difficult decisions on behalf of the district.
- Have knowledge and a working understanding of public education funding and demonstrated ability to manage budgets.
- A track record of successfully seeking and implementing best practices to maximize success of the organization.
- Expertise and knowledge in academic policy and pedagogy and the impact on student academic achievement (campus administration experience preferred).
- A leader who embraces and advances the district's innovative programs.
- Ability to communicate authentically and work collaboratively with the school board, district administrators, teachers, staff, parents, students, and other district constituents.
- A team builder who has the management style and interpersonal skills to hire, develop, motivate, and maintain a highly effective executive team and who can set clear expectations and delegate authority while remaining knowledgeable and accountable for the district's overall progress and activities.
- A role model for students and staff who demonstrates humility and exemplary moral character along with excellent people skills.
- An innovative problem-solver that is committed to work in partnership with the board of trustees to resolve district challenges.
- Demonstrates interest and a willingness to participate in community activities, organizations, and partnerships between the district and community.

Application Materials
Your application should include:

- Letter of Interest
- Current Resume

Copyright material from Gary E. Martin, Jimmy R. Creel, Thomas W. Harvey, Robert E. Nicks, and Michael Schwanenberger (2023), *District Leader Internship*, Routledge

- ◆ Brief Description of Major Accomplishments/Career/Academic Vita
- ◆ List of References
- ◆ Copies of Certification(s)
- ◆ Completed Copy of Verification Form

Sample Verification Form

Your initials in the space provided for each statement indicates that you agree with the statement. Please provide a brief explanation for any statement that you believe needs explanation.

_____ I have never been, nor am I currently the subject of an inquiry, review, or investigation for alleged misconduct or alleged violation of the professional standards of conduct.

_____ I have never failed to complete a contract for educational services in any educational or school district-related position for any alleged misconduct or alleged violation of professional standards of conduct.

_____ I have never surrendered a professional license of any kind before its expiration.

_____ I have never been disciplined by any public agency responsible for licensure of any kind, including but not limited to educational licensure.

_____ I have never been charged with a felony or misdemeanor such as: driving under the influence of intoxicants, alcohol, or illegal drugs.

_____ I have never had any civil complaint, judgment or other court order entered against me resulting from abuse, assault, battery, harassment, intimidation, neglect, stalking, or other threatening behavior toward other persons.

_____ I have never been the subject of a substantiated report of child abuse or sexual misconduct of any kind.

_____ I authorize this school district to make such investigations and inquiries of my personal, employment, educational, financial, and other related matters as may be necessary for an employment decision.

_____ I understand that any misrepresentation on this verification form may be grounds for employment dismissal if employed by the school district.

Sample Timeline

Month of September	Recruitment
October 1	Board receives top 15 applications for review
October 15	Board meeting to determine 1st round interviews
October 16	Consultant contacts applicants not selected for an interview
October 20–25	Board conducts 1st round interviews
October 30	Board meeting to identify 2nd round interviews
November 5–7	Board conducts 2nd round interviews
November 10	Board meeting to select new superintendent or in some states, will name lone finalist*

*Lone finalist is a designation used in some states in which the board may not hire the individual for 21 days while the district completes a background check and/or further review of the applicant.

Copyright material from Gary E. Martin, Jimmy R. Creel, Thomas W. Harvey, Robert E. Nicks, and Michael Schwanenberger (2023), *District Leader Internship*, Routledge

NELP/PSEL Standards
Appendix A.3 — Crosswalk

NELP Preparation Program Standards	**PSEL** Standards for Practicing School District Leaders
NELP Standard 1: Mission, Vision, and Improvement: To collaboratively lead, design, and implement a district mission, vision, and process for continuous improvement that reflects a core set of values and priorities that include data use, technology, values, equity, diversity, digital citizenship, and community.	
Component 1.1: Understand and demonstrate the capacity to collaboratively design, communicate, and evaluate a district mission and vision that reflects a core set of values and priorities that include data use, technology, values, equity, diversity, digital citizenship, and community.	1a. Develop an educational mission for the school to promote the academic success and well-being of each student. 1b. In collaboration with members of the school and the community and using relevant data, develop and promote a vision for the school on the successful learning and development of each child and on instructional and organizational practices that promote such success. 1c. Articulate, advocate, and cultivate core values that define the school's culture and stress the imperative of child-centered education; high expectations and student support; equity, inclusiveness, and social justice; openness, caring, and trust; and continuous improvement. 1d. Strategically develop, implement, and evaluate actions to achieve the vision for the school. 1e. Review the school's mission and vision and adjust them to changing expectations and opportunities for the school, and the changing needs and situations of students. 1f. Develop shared understanding of and commitment to mission, vision, and core values within the school and the community. 1g. Model and pursue the school's mission, vision, and core values in all aspects of leadership.

Copyright material from Gary E. Martin, Jimmy R. Creel, Thomas W. Harvey, Robert E. Nicks, and Michael Schwanenberger (2023), *District Leader Internship*, Routledge

Component 1.2: Understand and demonstrate the capacity to lead district strategic planning and continuous improvement processes that engage diverse stakeholders in data collection, diagnosis, design, implementation, and evaluation.	1d. Strategically develop, implement, and evaluate actions to achieve the vision for the school. 10a. Seek to make the school more effective for each student, teachers and staff, families, and the community. 10b. Use methods of continuous improvement to achieve the vision, fulfill the mission, and promote the core values of the school. 10d. Engage others in an ongoing process of evidence-based inquiry, learning, strategic goal setting, planning, implementation, and evaluation for continuous school and classroom improvement. 10g. Develop technically appropriate systems of data collection, management, analysis, and use, connecting as needed to the district office and external partners for support in planning, implementation, monitoring, feedback, and evaluation. 10h. Adopt a systems perspective and promote coherence among improvement efforts and all aspects of school organization, programs, and services. 10j. Develop and promote leadership among teachers and staff for inquiry, experimentation, and innovation, and initiating and implementing improvement.

Copyright material from Gary E. Martin, Jimmy R. Creel, Thomas W. Harvey, Robert E. Nicks, and Michael Schwanenberger (2023), *District Leader Internship*, Routledge

NELP District Standard 2: Ethics and Professional Norms: To advocate for ethical decisions and cultivate professional norms and culture.	
Component 2.1: Understand and demonstrate the capacity to reflect on, communicate about, and cultivate professional dispositions and norms (i.e., equity, fairness, integrity, transparency, trust, collaboration, perseverance, reflection, lifelong learning, digital citizenship) and professional district and school cultures.	2b. Act according to and promote the professional norms of integrity, fairness, transparency, trust, collaboration, perseverance, learning, and continuous improvement. 2c. Place children at the center of education and accept responsibility for each student's academic success and well-being. (Implicit in all standards.) 2d. Safeguard and promote the values of democracy, individual freedom and responsibility, equity, social justice, community, and diversity. 3g. Act with cultural competence and responsiveness in their interactions, decision making, and practice. 3h. Address matters of equity and cultural responsiveness in all aspects of leadership. 7c. Establish and sustain a professional culture of engagement and commitment to shared vision, goals, and objectives pertaining to the education of the whole child; high expectations for professional work; ethical and equitable practice; trust and open communication; and collaboration, collective efficacy, and continuous individual and organizational learning and improvement. 7d. Promote mutual accountability among teachers and other professional staff for each student's success and the effectiveness of the school as a whole. 7e. Develop and support open, productive, caring, and trusting working relationships among leaders, faculty, and staff to promote professional capacity and the improvement of practice. 7g. Provide opportunities for collaborative examination of practice, collegial feedback, and collective learning.
Component 2.2: Understand and demonstrate the capacity to evaluate and advocate for ethical and legal decisions.	9h. Know, comply with, and help the school community understand local, state, and federal laws, rights, policies, and regulations in order to promote student success.

Copyright material from Gary E. Martin, Jimmy R. Creel, Thomas W. Harvey, Robert E. Nicks, and Michael Schwanenberger (2023), *District Leader Internship*, Routledge

Component 2.3: Understand and demonstrate the capacity to model ethical behavior in their personal conduct and relationships and to cultivate ethical behavior in others.	2a. Act ethically and professionally in personal conduct, relationships with others, decision making, stewardship of the school's resources, and all aspects of school leadership. 2e. Lead with interpersonal and communication skill, social-emotional insight, and understanding of all students' and staff members' backgrounds and cultures. 2f. Provide moral direction for the school and promote ethical and professional behavior among faculty and staff.

Copyright material from Gary E. Martin, Jimmy R. Creel, Thomas W. Harvey, Robert E. Nicks, and Michael Schwanenberger (2023), *District Leader Internship*, Routledge

NELP District Standard 3: Equity, Inclusiveness, and Cultural Responsiveness:
To develop and maintain a supportive, equitable, culturally responsive, and inclusive district culture.

Component 3.1: Understand and demonstrate the capacity to evaluate, cultivate, and advocate for a supportive and inclusive district culture.	3g. Act with cultural competence and responsiveness in their interactions, decision making, and practice. 5a. Build and maintain a safe, caring, and healthy school environment that meets the academic, social, emotional, and physical needs of each student. 5b. Create and sustain a school environment in which each student is known, accepted and valued, trusted and respected, cared for, and encouraged to be an active and responsible member of the school community. 5d. Promote adult-student, student-peer, and school-community relationships that value and support academic learning and positive social and emotional development. 5f. Infuse the school's learning environment with the cultures and languages of the school's community
Component 3.2: Understand and demonstrate the capacity to evaluate, cultivate, and advocate for equitable access to safe and nurturing schools and the opportunities and resources, including instructional materials, technologies, classrooms teachers, interventions, and adult relationships, necessary to support the success and well-being of each student.	3c. Ensure that each student has equitable access to effective teachers, learning opportunities, academic and social support, and other resources necessary for success. 3d. Develop student policies and address student misconduct in a positive, fair, and unbiased manner. 3e. Confront and alter institutional biases of student marginalization, deficit-based schooling, and low expectations associated with race, class, culture and language, gender, and sexual orientation, and disability or special status. 3h. Address matters of equity and cultural responsiveness in all aspects of leadership.
Component 3.3: Understand and demonstrate the capacity to evaluate, advocate, and cultivate equitable, inclusive, and culturally responsive instructional and behavior support practices among teachers and staff.	3g. Act with cultural competence and responsiveness in their interactions, decision making, and practice. 3h. Address matters of equity and cultural responsiveness in all aspects of leadership. 7b. Empower and entrust teachers and staff with collective responsibility for meeting the academic, social, emotional, and physical needs of each student, pursuant to the mission, vision, and core values of the school.

Copyright material from Gary E. Martin, Jimmy R. Creel, Thomas W. Harvey, Robert E. Nicks, and Michael Schwanenberger (2023), *District Leader Internship*, Routledge

NELP District Standard 4: Learning and Instruction: To evaluate, design, cultivate, and implement coherent systems of curriculum, instruction, supports, assessment, and instructional leadership.

Component 4.1: Understand and can demonstrate the capacity to evaluate, design, and implement high-quality curricula, the use of technology, and other services and supports for academic and non-academic student programs.	4c. Promote instructional practice that is consistent with knowledge of child learning and development, effective pedagogy, and the needs of each student. 4d. Ensure instructional practice that is intellectually challenging, authentic to student experiences, recognizes student strengths, and is differentiated and personalized. 4e. Promote the effective use of technology in the service of teaching and learning. 5c. Provide coherent systems of academic and social supports, services, extracurricular activities, and accommodations to meet the range of learning needs of each student.
Component 4.2: Understand and can demonstrate the capacity to collaboratively evaluate, design, and cultivate coherent systems of support, coaching, and professional development for educators, educational professionals, and school and district leaders, including themselves, that promote reflection, digital literacy, distributed leadership, data literacy, equity, improvement, and student success.	3h. Address matters of equity and cultural responsiveness in all aspects of leadership. 6g. Develop the capacity, opportunities, and support for teacher leadership and leadership from other members of the school community.
Component 4.3: Understand and can demonstrate the capacity to design, implement, and evaluate a developmentally appropriate, accessible, and culturally responsive system of assessments and data collection, management, and analysis that support instructional improvement, equity, student learning and wellbeing, and instructional leadership.	3g. Act with cultural competence and responsiveness in their interactions, decision making, and practice. 3h. Address matters of equity and cultural responsiveness in all aspects of leadership. 4f. Employ valid assessments that are consistent with knowledge of child learning and development and technical standards of measurement. 4g. Use assessment data appropriately and within technical limitations to monitor student progress and improve instruction.

Copyright material from Gary E. Martin, Jimmy R. Creel, Thomas W. Harvey, Robert E. Nicks, and Michael Schwanenberger (2023), *District Leader Internship*, Routledge

Component 4.4: Understand and demonstrate the capacity to design, implement, and evaluate district-wide use of coherent systems of curriculum, instruction, assessment, student services, technology, and instructional resources that support the needs of each student in the district.	4a. Implement coherent systems of curriculum, instruction, and assessment that promote the mission, vision, and core values of the school, embody high expectations for student learning, align with academic standards, and are culturally responsive. 4b. Align and focus systems of curriculum, instruction, and assessment within and across grade levels to promote student academic success, love of learning, the identities and habits of learners, and healthy sense of self

Copyright material from Gary E. Martin, Jimmy R. Creel, Thomas W. Harvey, Robert E. Nicks, and Michael Schwanenberger (2023), *District Leader Internship*, Routledge

NELP District Standard 5: Community and External Leadership: To understand and engage families, communities, and other constituents in the work of schools and the district and to advocate for district, student, and community needs.	
Component 5.1: Understand and demonstrate the capacity to represent and support district schools in engaging diverse families in strengthening student learning in and out of school.	3b. Recognize, respect, and employ each student's strengths, diversity, and culture as assets for teaching and learning. 3g. Act with cultural competence and responsiveness in their interactions, decision making, and practice. 8a. Are approachable, accessible, and welcoming to families and members of the community. 8b. Create and sustain positive, collaborative, and productive relationships with families and the community for the benefit of students. 8c. Engage in regular and open two-way communication with families and the community about the school, students, needs, problems, and accomplishments.
Component 5.2: Understand and demonstrate the capacity to understand, engage and effectively collaborate and communicate with, through oral, written, and digital means, diverse families, community members, partners, and other constituencies to benefit students, schools, and the district as a whole.	3b. Recognize, respect, and employ each student's strengths, diversity, and culture as assets for teaching and learning. 3g. Act with cultural competence and responsiveness in their interactions, decision making, and practice. 8b. Create and sustain positive, collaborative, and productive relationships with families and the community for the benefit of students. 8c. Engage in regular and open two-way communication with families and the community about the school, students, needs, problems, and accomplishments. 8d. Maintain a presence in the community to understand its strengths and needs, develop productive relationships, and engage its resources for the school. 8e. Create means for the school community to partner with families to support student learning in and out of school. 8f. Understand, value, and employ the community's cultural, social, intellectual, and political resources to promote student learning and school improvement. 8j. Build and sustain productive partnerships with the public and private sectors to promote school improvement and student learning.

Copyright material from Gary E. Martin, Jimmy R. Creel, Thomas W. Harvey, Robert E. Nicks, and Michael Schwanenberger (2023), *District Leader Internship*, Routledge

Component 5.3: Understand and demonstrate the capacity to communicate through oral, written, and digital means within the larger organizational, community, and political contexts and cultivate relationships with members of the business, civic, and policy community in support of their advocacy for district, school, student, and community needs.	8h. Advocate for the school and district and for the importance of education and student needs and priorities to families and the community. 8i. Advocate publicly for the needs and priorities of students, families, and the community. 8j. Build and sustain productive partnerships with the public and private sectors to promote school improvement and student learning

Copyright material from Gary E. Martin, Jimmy R. Creel, Thomas W. Harvey, Robert E. Nicks, and Michael Schwanenberger (2023), *District Leader Internship*, Routledge

NELP District Standard 6: Operations and Management: To develop, monitor, evaluate, and manage district systems for operations, resources, technology, and human capital management.

Component 6.1: Understand and demonstrate the capacity to develop, communicate, implement, and evaluate data-informed and equitable management, communication, technology, governance, and operation systems at the district level to support schools in realizing the district's mission and vision.	4e. Promote the effective use of technology in the service of teaching and learning. 9a. Institute, manage, and monitor operations and administrative systems that promote the mission and vision of the school. 9b. Strategically manage staff resources, assigning and scheduling teachers and staff to roles and responsibilities that optimize their professional capacity to address each student's learning needs. 9f. Employ technology to improve the quality and efficiency of operations and management. 9g. Develop and maintain data and communication systems to deliver actionable information for classroom and school improvement.
Component 6.2: Understand and demonstrate the capacity to develop, communicate, implement and evaluate a data-based district resourcing plan and support schools in developing their school level resourcing plans.	3h. Address matters of equity and cultural responsiveness in all aspects of leadership. 9c. Seek, acquire, and manage fiscal, physical, and other resources to support curriculum, instruction, and assessment; the student learning community; professional capacity and community; and family and community engagement. 9d. Are responsible, ethical, and accountable stewards of the school's monetary and nonmonetary resources, engaging in effective budgeting and accounting practices.

Copyright material from Gary E. Martin, Jimmy R. Creel, Thomas W. Harvey, Robert E. Nicks, and Michael Schwanenberger (2023), *District Leader Internship*, Routledge

Component 6.3: Understand and demonstrate the capacity to develop, implement, and evaluate coordinated, data-informed systems for hiring, retaining, supervising, and developing school and district staff in order to support the district's collective instructional and leadership capacity.	6a. Recruit, hire, support, develop, and retain effective and caring teachers and other professional staff and form them into an educationally effective faculty. 6b. Plan for and manage staff turnover and succession, providing opportunities for effective induction and mentoring of new personnel. 6c. Develop teachers' and staff members' professional knowledge, skills, and practice through differentiated opportunities for learning and growth, guided by understanding of professional and adult learning and development. 6d. Foster continuous improvement of individual and collective instructional capacity to achieve outcomes envisioned for each student. 6e. Deliver actionable feedback about instruction and other professional practice through valid, research-anchored systems of supervision and evaluation to support the development of teachers' and staff members' knowledge, skills, and practice. 6f. Empower and motivate teachers and staff to the highest levels of professional practice and to continuous learning and improvement. 7a. Develop workplace conditions for teachers and other professional staff that promote effective professional development, practice, and student learning. 7f. Design and implement job-embedded and other opportunities for collaborative professional learning with faculty and staff.

Copyright material from Gary E. Martin, Jimmy R. Creel, Thomas W. Harvey, Robert E. Nicks, and Michael Schwanenberger (2023), *District Leader Internship*, Routledge

NELP District Standard 7: Policy Governance and Advocacy: To cultivate relationships, lead collaborative decision-making and governance, and represent and advocate for district needs in broader policy conversations.	
Component 7.1: Understand and demonstrate the capacity to represent the district, advocate for district needs, and cultivate a respectful and responsive relationship with the district's board of education focused on achieving the shared mission	8h. Advocate for the school and district, and for the importance of education and student needs and priorities, to families and the community. 8i. Advocate publicly for the needs and priorities of students, families, and the community
Component 7.2: Understand and demonstrate the capacity to design, implement, cultivate, and evaluate effective and collaborative systems for district governance that engage multiple and diverse stakeholder groups, including school and district personnel, families, community stakeholders, and board members.	9i. Develop and manage relationships with feeder and connecting schools for enrollment management and curricular and instructional articulation. 10c. Prepare the school and the community for improvement, promoting readiness, an imperative for improvement, instilling mutual commitment and accountability, and developing the knowledge, skills, and motivation to succeed in improvement
Component 7.3: Understand and demonstrate the capacity to evaluate, engage in decision making around, implement, and appropriately communicate about district, state, and national policy, laws, rules, and regulations.	9g. Know, comply with, and help the school community understand local, state, and federal laws, rights, policies, and regulations, in order to promote student success.
Component 7.4: Understand the implications of larger cultural, social, economic, legal, and political interests, changes, and expectations and demonstrate the capacity to evaluate and represent district needs and priorities within larger policy conversations and advocate for the needs and priorities of the district at the local, state, and national level.	N/A

Source: NPBEA (2018). National Educational Leadership Preparation (NELP) Program Recognition Standards – District Level, p. 120–133. Retrieved from: www.npbea.org.

Copyright material from Gary E. Martin, Jimmy R. Creel, Thomas W. Harvey, Robert E. Nicks, and Michael Schwanenberger (2023), *District Leader Internship*, Routledge

References

Burry, M. (2018, April 29). The Balance Careers. Retrieved from Job Resumes: https://www.thebalancecareers.com/job-resumes-4161923

Corda, S. (2012, March). Crafting the Resume. Principal: National Association of Elementary Principals, 2. Retrieved from https://www-naesp-org.libproxy.lamar.edu/resources-principal-marchapril-2012/practitioners-corner-crafting-r-sum-2

Copyright material from Gary E. Martin, Jimmy R. Creel, Thomas W. Harvey, Robert E. Nicks, and Michael Schwanenberger (2023), *District Leader Internship*, Routledge

■ Index